CARY GRANT
A CELEBRATION OF STYLE

CARY GRANT
A CELEBRATION OF STYLE

Richard Torregrossa

Foreword by Giorgio Armani
Afterword by Michael Kors

BULFINCH PRESS
NEW YORK BOSTON

Bulfinch Press

Hachette Book Group USA
1271 Avenue of the Americas, New York, NY 10020
Visit our Web site at www.bulfinchpress.com

First Edition: September 2006

Library of Congress Cataloging-in-Publication Data

Torregrossa, Richard.
  Cary Grant : a celebration of style / Richard Torregrossa.
     p. cm.
ISBN-10: 0-8212-5760-9 (hardcover)
ISBN-13: 978-0-8212-5760-9 (hardcover)
1. Grant, Cary, 1904–1986 2. Motion picture actors and actresses — United States — Biography. I. Title.

PN2287.G675T67 2006
791.4302'8092 — dc22   2005031265

Design by Joel Avirom, Jason Snyder, and Meghan Day Healey

PRINTED IN SINGAPORE

"Style begins and ends with Cary Grant."

—Alan Flusser

CONTENTS

THERE'S A FUNNY THING about names—sometimes they fit, and sometimes they don't. I've never really given changing my name much thought, as I am told that *Giorgio Armani* is the kind of name you expect an Italian fashion designer to have. But had I been called the Italian equivalent of Archibald Alexander Leach, I may well have considered swapping it. This is precisely what Cary Grant did, and you can see why—the smooth, debonair, and, above all, elegant actor was so much more a *Cary Grant* than an *Archie Leach*, though the name he was born with might have done for his appearances in those celebrated screwball comedies of the thirties and forties, like *Bringing Up Baby* and *His Girl Friday*. But even when he was playing for laughs, he still managed to be effortlessly stylish and—that word again—elegant. It is this quality that I marvel at and which for me makes him a great male role model.

In my designs, I see elegance as the most important quality as it gives the wearer confidence and the look of someone not trying too hard. Cary Grant managed to give great performances in comedies, thrillers, and romances (and often appeared in films that combined all three genres, like *To Catch a Thief*), and at all times he appeared cool and immaculate. He had an easy manner, his ready wit and charm complemented by his ability to wear clothes effortlessly. Cary Grant always looks relaxed in his stylish outfits. So great a talent as well as an incredibly handsome man—no wonder he became a screen idol. As he once said: "Everyone wants to be Cary Grant: even I want to be Cary Grant."

"Our dreams are our real life." —FEDERICO FELLINI

IN THE BEVERLY HILLS HOTEL, there is a fittingly larger-than-life photograph of Cary Grant behind a glass display case. He's wearing a chalk-stripe suit and a shirt that is as white and dazzling as his smile. Underneath the photograph is a tuxedo, an unfurled bow tie, cuff links, and a pair of carefully placed polished shoes. It's an advertisement for Amir, the menswear showroom in the corridor of swanky shops on the lower level of the hotel, but it's more than just an advertisement—it's an homage, less a display case than a kind of altar. A placard in the case bears the inscription "This is a tribute to my friend Mr. Cary Grant who had style. His style was simply understated elegance." ▪ Recently Giorgio Armani said that his "overall sense of style as a designer has been greatly influenced by Cary Grant in the Hitchcock classics *Notorious* and *North by Northwest.*" ▪ Although Cary Grant has not been with us for many years—2006 marks the twentieth anniversary of his death—he is seemingly everywhere, not only in those wonderful old movies but as a joyful spirit, his influence as strong and as palpable as ever, inspiring us to dress better, to behave better, and ultimately, to live better.

CARY GRANT began his career as a vaudevillian acrobat, a teenager tumbling his way across Roaring Twenties America before he made the tough transition to Broadway star. In 1932 he moved to Hollywood, where he became a kind of "Valentino without a horse." Appearances in two Mae West sex farces brought him international fame as the new hunk of the month, a fan rave. Good reviews in a string of flops with Katharine Hepburn saved his career and

"There's a very interesting, sort of dark side, to almost all of Grant's characterizations. Even his comedies, for which he's obviously best known, have a touch of darkness and mystery to them. That's what made him better than other guys who were doing it in the great age of romantic comedies."
—RICHARD SCHICKEL

showed audiences—and more importantly, producers—that he was as talented as he was handsome. The movie in which we see the first glimmer of the Cary Grant style was *The Awful Truth* (1937), with Irene Dunne, a screwball comedy that filmmaker and historian Peter Bogdanovich says was "the birth of the Cary Grant we came to know and love."

The Awful Truth was followed by some of Cary Grant's most memorable collaborations with directors Hawks and Hitchcock, Cukor and McCarey, and later Stanley Donen, in which he branded the Cary Grant persona with a thrilling signature style—"James Bond without a gun," as one critic put it.

To be sure his career was an extraordinary one, and it has yet to be rivaled; it spanned more than three decades and produced seventy-two films, many of them classics, many of them more popular today than they were when they were first released, and every one of them moneymakers.

"The amazing thing about Cary Grant," says Los Angeles fashion designer Amir, "is that he maintained it offscreen as well as on. It was not a disposable image or a persona created by a studio or stylist."

At sixty-two he retired a wealthy man, long before he had to, still in demand—and he would be until his dying day, a top box-office draw, older but never old.

The rise of Cary Grant the movie star has been well documented by many biographers and film historians, but there is one aspect of his extraordinary life and career that has been largely overlooked—his enduring influence as a man of style, a fashion icon. I'm talking about style not only in the sense of how he wore his Savile Row suits, but style as a revelation of character, as a way of facing the world, a means by which all of life's riches are embraced and celebrated. As former Gucci creative director Tom Ford once said, "For me, fashion doesn't stop at clothes. Fashion is everything: art, music, design, graphic design, hair, makeup, architecture, the way cars look—all those things go together to make a moment in time."

The story that hasn't been told is how Cary Grant created Cary Grant—the consummate leading man, loved by women, admired by men—a star whose style is timeless, as appealing today as it was back in Hollywood's golden era.

He certainly wasn't born that way. Far from it. On January 18, 1904, Cary Grant entered the world at 1:00 a.m. as Archibald Leach, a poor boy from a provincial town in England, the other side of the world from Hollywood, both literally and figuratively. He was the only son of a pants presser and a strict mother who disappeared from his life when he was nine, only to addle him with a startling reappearance twenty years later.

CG style from head to hose.

Cary Grant and Irene Dunne snuggle up in Penny Serenade *(1941).*

At sixteen he left home, never to return (except for brief visits), a kind of Dickensian waif wandering the world undaunted by what could not have been a more uncertain or dismal-seeming future. He had only a minimal education and no skills, no recognizable talent, and certainly no money, no connections, no rich uncle secretly supporting him, no one to look after him except himself. In many ways he was dangerously and at times tragically alone, "a street fighter," as one of his former wives called him. He was the least likely person to become a genteel model of manners, the ne plus ultra of style and elegance, or as Pauline Kael put it, "the Man from Dream City."

Yet in an astonishingly short period of time, he created a dazzling screen image and signature style that is still revered today.

"The amazing thing about Cary Grant," says Los Angeles fashion designer Amir, whose clients include Brad Pitt, Prince Charles, and former president Bill Clinton, "is that he maintained it offscreen as well as on. It was not a disposable image or a persona created by a studio or stylist. He put his whole heart and soul into it, like a work of art. He *was* a work of art. No one has ever quite done that since."

"He's still the height of romance," says Pamela Fiori, editor in chief of *Town & Country* magazine. "We're still in love with him, still trying to figure out how he did it, and loving every minute of it."

Grant was a man of character as well as a man of style. Hitchcock biographer Donald Spoto met Grant when Hitchcock received his Lifetime Achievement Award, in 1979 at the Beverly Hilton Hotel. Says Spoto:

"Cary was in such good humor. He was charming; he was funny; he was Cary Grant! The only difference was that in his on-screen persona he rarely laughed out loud or had big emotional scenes; everything was downplayed, which was one of the things that made him one of the most brilliant actors in the history of film, totally unacknowledged, totally underrated. But you can see it in films like *Penny Serenade*, in which he gives one of the greatest performances ever put on film, or *Holiday*, *Bringing Up Baby*, or *None but the Lonely Heart*. The ultimate demonstration of his dignity, his humor, his character is the fact that throughout these decades of brilliant performances and hard work, during which he mastered his craft, he never once complained that he wasn't getting his due, that he didn't get an Oscar for this or that performance, that he wasn't getting award dinners. People think they're only complaining today. Oh, they complained back then, but he never did. He was a great, great actor, and I think that needs to be said."

Clearly, Cary Grant still matters.

But the question remains: how did Archie Leach become Cary Grant? In an era of makeover mania, cosmetic enhancements, and de rigueur reinvention, no question could be more intriguingly relevant.

"That is the profounder question," says film historian David Thomson. "Where did it all come from? That voice—neither American nor British. A lot of the English actors like Ronald Coleman never changed their accent. Coleman has a distinctly British accent. Grant definitely does something to his voice. Did he go to elocution classes? Did he work on it? It's a fascinating thing, because it becomes a voice that belongs not quite anywhere. He's unique in so many ways."

And what about his sartorial eloquence, for which he is so highly regarded among the fashion-conscious as well as fans? He surely didn't learn it in the

> *"Style is a magic wand, and turns everything to gold that it touches."*
> —LOGAN PEARSALL SMITH

rough-and-tumble streets of working-class Bristol. Audrey Hepburn had Givenchy, Jackie Kennedy had Oleg Cassini and Halston, but who showed Cary Grant the way to Savile Row?

Sylvester Stallone, the street tough from Hell's Kitchen, is not that far a stretch to Rocky or Rambo. The terribly British characters Hugh Grant plays so brilliantly in all those fluffy Richard Curtis comedies are not a far cry from his Oxford (or is it Cambridge?) origins.

But Archie Leach to Cary Grant? It's akin to Arnold Schwarzenegger creating Quentin Crisp or Robert Blake inventing Mr. Rogers. Mathematically, it just doesn't add up; the end result seems to defy the laws of physics. Cary Grant did more than just "make something of himself"; he made something *else* of himself, a truly unique accomplishment as well as a very modern ambition.

"Nowadays we've had a lot more experience with people who have made that kind of journey," says Thomson. "But he was a pioneer."

His story, then, is about so much more than clever careerism, so much more than just another rags-to-riches tale, another real-life Runyonesque yarn in which the protagonist starts low and ends high by dint of sheer grit and determination. Surely he had those qualities, but the story of Cary Grant is about the power of personal transformation, from which we can all learn. It's an especially meaningful lesson in an age in which where we begin in life seems to be the last place we want to end up, no matter how good we have it.

As we shall see, Grant's personal style evolved as much from his flaws as his flawlessness, as much from what he didn't wear as what he did wear, as much from his failures as his successes.

The style he created was not just an appealing facade. It went deep into the heart and soul of who he was and whom he wanted to become. And it was not always smooth sailing. As he himself said, "I spent the greater part of my life fluctuating between Archie Leach and Cary Grant, unsure of either, suspecting each."

It is a great irony that the man who has come to represent perfection in so many areas of life was himself imperfect, certainly as human as the rest of us—which is one reason why he touches audiences so deeply and why his evolution is as instructive as it is inspiring.

Revealing the style secrets of an icon might seem like a coldly clinical exercise. No doubt, he would have hated it, for he was an intensely private man.

But after we shine the light upon the magic, we find that he loses none of his allure. In fact he only gains from it. Behind the iconic man of style was a profoundly moral being whose love of life and infectious joy still enrich us today. As Ralph Lauren has said, "If you wanted to be happy you would go to a Cary Grant movie."

This, then, is a celebration of not only a remarkable talent but a remarkable man. And how could anyone, Cary Grant included, object to that?

"You can learn more by watching Cary Grant drink a cup of coffee than by spending six months with a Method actor."
— Tony Curtis

CARY GRANT
A CELEBRATION OF STYLE

ONE

DRESSED TO KILL

"My idea of a well-dressed guy was General MacArthur."
— GLENN O'BRIEN, *THE STYLE GUY*

I T IS THE SUMMER of 1932, and although the country is in the throes of the Great Depression, the Paramount lot is bustling. Powerful producers and bit players, stars and starlets hastily make their way from the sound stages to the commissary for a much-needed lunch break.

The days here are long; shooting begins at dawn and doesn't end until well after dark, so the actors and actresses, some still in full makeup and period costumes—oh, *look*, there's Louis XIV and Marie Antoinette, a gaggle of giggling chorines, and two clowns talking to a countess!—fuel up on coffee, lots and lots of coffee. They'll need it. Some of them will work on one picture during the day, another at night.

Although Paramount is on the verge of bankruptcy, the sun shines on it from an unblemished blue sky, bathing it in a heavenly light, and the air glitters like sparkles dropped from a balloon. After all this is Hollywood, the land of mirth and magic, happy endings and pleasant dreams, the home of heartthrob Gary Cooper and the Marx Brothers, gunslinger Wild Bill Cody and glamour girls Greta Garbo and Jean Harlow. There are no dark clouds here, none that are visible anyway, for none are allowed. Instead there's an energy in the air, an excitement, an optimism, an

Cary Grant in 1932's Madame Butterfly, *one of seven movies he made during his first year under contract at Paramount.*

intense determination. Perhaps that's why the scene is so charged. Everybody is moving at full tilt, amped-up on high hopes and caffeine or, if necessary, Benzedrine—whatever it takes to get the job done, for the future is uncertain. The studio is literally just one box-office failure away from ruin. You could be an extra in a movie with Clark Gable one day, standing in a breadline the next. It could go either way.

But there is one young man who stands apart and yet is a part of it all. His face is upturned, tilted toward the sun, absorbing as much of its warmth as he can before he departs for his next assignment on Soundstage 7, where he'll likely be laboring under hot kliegs, tripping over sound cables, and kowtowing to barking directors on an airless set until long after sunset.

He's smiling, optimistic, upbeat. Perhaps it's the rejuvenating effects of the sun; perhaps it's the costume, an immaculate naval uniform. Clothes, he has learned, instill confidence, and this is one spotless set of dress whites. His white naval uniform, like his smile, seems not to reflect the abundant California sunshine—untainted by exhaust and smog in those days—but to exude it. There is something radiant about him. At six feet two inches, 180 pounds, he's tall and trim, robustly tan, and fit; he cuts quite a dashing figure, which is, after all, why they hired him.

The young man is barely twenty-eight years old, and his name is Cary Grant. But he's not quite Cary Grant yet, at least not the Cary Grant we've come to know and love, the icon we celebrate today, the lovable lout in *The Philadelphia Story*, the gorgeous goofball in *Bringing Up Baby*, the irresistible playboy in *An Affair to Remember*, the cynosure of style in *To Catch a Thief*, the advertising executive turned sexy superhero in *North by Northwest*, or the movie star of movie stars who perfected charm and elegance with such ease that he fooled us all into thinking that we could do it, too, as if it was as simple as learning a card trick.

At this moment, though, he's neither newcomer nor novice, certainly not an extra, but by no means a major star. He's something in between, a contract player, earning $450 per week, a princely sum in those days; it's more than enough to afford him the luxe life—which includes a spacious Santa Monica beach house and a fancy sports car, a quince-colored Packard Coupe 8 roadster—but he's no Gary Cooper; far from it. He's appeared in eight movies and worked with one of Hollywood's best directors (Joseph von Sternberg) and some of Hollywood's most prized leading ladies

Cary Grant and Marlene Dietrich in Blonde Venus *(1932). Dietrich called him "Hollywood's only true prince."*

(Carole Lombard, Marlene Dietrich), but the parts have been small. Fact is, he's disposable, one of many contract players on the lot scrambling for better roles, still a cog in a very lucrative but dicey wheel. It could all end tomorrow.

Still, an aura surrounds him, the kind of glow that is produced by those rare moments when we find ourselves exactly where we want to be and know exactly where we're going.

And someone notices it, someone very important.

Just as Grant is about to go on his way, he catches the eye of one of Paramount's newest stars, Mae West, as she alights from her chauffeured automobile. She glances across the lot, past the surging throng of hobos and harlots, glamour girls and costumed courtiers, and sees him as if by chance but what we now know was fate.

> *"If he can talk . . .*
> *I want him in*
> *my picture."*
> —Mae West

She is struck by his looks, the way he seems to glisten like a saber in the sunlight. Mae West knows a handsome hunk when she sees one, and she does not hesitate. "If he can talk," she says to William LeBaron, her producer, "I want him in my picture."

And it is done. The break that many up-and-comers lie awake at night dreaming about has befallen Cary Grant—although he doesn't know it yet.

Mae West is Paramount's lucrative light, their box-office hopeful. A lot is riding on her first feature film, *She Done Him Wrong*, a comedy based on her hit Broadway play, *Diamond Lil*. It's chock-full of daring double entendres and saucy songs like "I Like A Guy What Takes His Time," which are much loved by depressed Depression-era audiences. And Mae West does not disappoint.

For this role Grant dutifully slips out of his sailor suit and into another uniform, that of a Salvation Army captain, and plays straight man to Mae West's bawdy brand of comedy. "Do you mind if I get personal?" asks a wary and very stiff-looking CG, as if he's afraid his lecherous leading lady might swallow him whole. The predatory West replies, "I don't mind if you get familiar."

The movie is a huge hit, and everything changes: Mae West's star rises even higher, Paramount is pulled back from the brink of bankruptcy, and Cary Grant is adored by a worldwide audience and goes on to become, well, Cary Grant.

THE FACT THAT the man who would come to embody the sartorial gold standard was wearing a uniform that fateful day is a clue to the stylistic eloquence with which he would be associated for the rest of his life.

In 1917 Archie joined the Bristol Boy Scouts, then in its infancy. He was thirteen, athletic, energetic, and like most teenagers, a little restless. "I welcomed any occupation," he recalled, "that promised activity."

He was also unhappy at home. His mother, Elsie, he had been told, had gone to "the seaside for a holiday." But that had been three years prior. "I realized at some point that she wasn't coming back." The power of this incident cannot be underestimated, for it would haunt him for the rest of his life.

His mother had reputedly suffered a mental breakdown and was institutionalized at the behest of his father, Elias Leach, who became involved with another woman. Soon after, Archie's step-brother was born.

The circumstances of Elsie's abrupt departure were never explained to Archie. He had returned home from school one day, and she was gone. He was only ten years old. He would not see her again for more than twenty years, when assuming she had abandoned him forever or had died long ago, he received a letter from a London solicitor informing him that not only was his mother still alive but that she was in good health, physically at least, and living at Fishponds, a sanatorium just a short distance from where he had romped and roamed as a Boy Scout in Bristol. She had been there all these years.

The letter had been prompted by his father's death, on December 1, 1935, caused by "extreme toxicity" or, as Grant would put it, "a slow breaking heart." The care of Elsie Leach fell to her son.

But Archie Leach was now Cary Grant, a rich and famous film star living six thousand miles away in Hollywood, "known to the world but not to my mother."

Why his father had never told him the truth about Elsie remains a mystery, but what is certain is that, despite the shocking turn of events, Cary Grant lovingly cared for his mother for the rest of her life, visiting her often in England, where she preferred to remain in familiar surroundings instead of at a hilltop house in Beverly Hills amid the orange blossoms and palm trees.

Although she was probably mentally ill, she had her lucid moments, during which they resumed their mother-and-son relationship to the best of their abilities.

She lived for the next forty-three years in comfort, showered by gifts and affection from her famous son, until her death, in 1973 at the age of ninety-six, when she peacefully slipped away in her sleep after her customary afternoon tea.

"I was so often alone and unsettled at home," Grant said of the years just following his mother's departure. With a new family and a laborious job, his father had little time to play cricket with him or take him to the shows at the Bristol Hippodrome as they had done before. Archie was raised as much by his kindly aunts and uncles as he was by his father. Shuttled from one house to another, he was unsure of where he belonged.

But the Boy Scouts welcomed him with open arms. The camaraderie of mates like Bob Bennett—who many decades later fondly recalled the fun they had playing "wide games," a sort of British version of flag football—and the guidance of his kindly Scout master, L. E. Grogan, who said that the troop was "the finest and largest troop in the area, about one hundred and fifty scouts," served as a refuge from a fractured and confusing home life.

The Scouts became a surrogate family for Archie, and their uniforms, with their polished badges, colorful patches, and special status, came to represent the fond familial security he never really experienced in Picton Street, the site of the house where he hoped in vain to live again with his mother and father.

At first his uniforms were a bit sloppy, but he soon learned to care for them with the respect his superiors demanded. Later in life he would take the same pains with the Kilgour suits and Turnbull & Asser custom-made shirts he stored in specially made closets and cupboards in his Beverly Hills home.

The Boy Scout uniform marks his earliest encounter with the pride and self-confidence to be derived from being properly attired, and it would exert a strong influence on him for the rest of his life.

There was another kind of uniform that was equally, if not more, influential on the impressionable young boy. A war was on. The Great War. Suddenly there were soldiers everywhere. Military bands, rowdy regiments, and dress parades enlivened the usually quiet streets of the small town seated on the Avon River.

It was an exciting time for a young boy. Not yet of military age, he patriotically volunteered to serve as a junior air-raid warden, messenger, and guide at the Southampton Docks, a post he received by virtue of his experience as a Boy Scout. The job gave him access to a restricted area and an up-close view of fighting men carrying kits and rifles who were shuttled onto crowded ships headed across the English Channel to bloody battlefields.

He saw thousands of young men board transport ships bound for France knowing full well that many of them would fall victim to enemy submarines trolling the English Channel before they even reached the battlefront.

His duties on the docks included running errands and giving each soldier a life preserver before he boarded ship. The soldiers offered him tips for his services. usually a few bob. a useful bit of change for a scruffy young lad in those days. but he declined any cash payment. accepting instead a shiny military button or a braided regimental badge from the soldiers. In fact he preferred it. These items became prized mementos. and he amassed quite a collection of them. Some he would keep for the rest of his life as proud relics of the youthful contribution he had made to the war effort; they became poignant reminders of the soldiers he had helped who were far less fortunate than he.

The military uniform. all uniforms. from then on came to hold complex associations for him—not only of danger. sadness. loss. and the pity of war but also the more noble ideals of courage. self-sacrifice. duty. and honor. as well as the boyish notions of adventure and romance.

"Gentlemen's clothes are a symbol of the power that man must hold and that passes from race to race."
—F. Scott Fitzgerald

When later in life he put on a uniform for heroic roles in war-themed movies such as *Gunga Din*, *The Last Outpost*, *Destination Tokyo*, and *Operation Petticoat*, his biggest hit, it was more than just a costume. The gear of the soldier had real meaning to him.

Although he would never serve in the military himself, he actively supported Allied efforts during World War II by performing for the troops and donating large sums of money to British war relief, including his entire salary from *The Philadelphia Story* and *Arsenic and Old Lace*. Five of Grant's cousins were killed in the bombing of Britain by German air raids.

Cynics say his largesse was merely a convenient tax write-off, but he could have given the money to any number of worthy charities or sought financial relief in tax shelters. In 1952, when Grant took a much-needed break from decades of nearly nonstop work and embarked on a round-the-world vacation with his third wife, Betsy Drake, he found time to visit hospitals filled with soldiers wounded in the Korean War.

UNIFORMS ALSO impressed him in another way. He learned early on that technically the military uniform is the apex of all attire. It is everything civilian clothing aspires to be: decorative as well as decorous, functional as well as flattering, dignified as well as daring, perfectly cut as well as comfortable. It can work wonders on a man (or woman), turning a weakling into a warrior, a coward into a combatant, a bum into a Beau Brummel. Clothes are the raw material of self-creation.

The precision cut of military garments made during World War I greatly influenced civilian dress. In fact then, as now, they might very well be the clothing designer's richest source of ideas and inspiration.

In 1920 Coco Chanel based her wide-legged "yachting pants" for women on sailor's bell-bottoms. The double-breasted jacket is really a cleverly altered eight-buttoned British naval coat. Wristwatches were a World War I innovation, a speedier way of noting the time when bullets were whizzing overhead than fishing in vests for pocket watches.

To this day the buttons on a man's jacket are on the right side, a feature originally designed to make it easier for soldiers to draw their swords, which were situated on the left. Women's coats fasten the opposite way, creating a kind of sartorial yin and yang.

There is scarcely an item of modern dress that does not have combative antecedents, including the men's necktie, which dates back to the early seventeenth century, when the distinctive neckwear of Croatian soldiers, conquering heroes of the Thirty Years' War, were adapted by fashionable French civilians.

The classic garment favored by both men and women that probably has the most pugnacious pedigree is the trench coat, or mackintosh, which was standard issue for the soldiers who fought in the slaughter of World War I. Bogart never looked quite so tough and Mitchum never quite so mighty as they did in their macs. Designers have never been able to resist the trench coat's unique blend of form and function, recasting it each season in various cuts and colors, shapes and lengths, but never losing sight of its battlefield origins.

"We have recruited so much of the modern wardrobe from the military in tailored valor, the pragmatism of warfare, and the memory of victory," explained Richard Martin, former curator of the Costume Institute at the Metropolitan Museum of Art in New York, "that it is hard to imagine modern dress without the presence of military adaptations."

The diagonal-striped tie introduced by Brooks Brothers in 1920 was inspired by the British "regimental" tie. It now hangs from the necks of hawks and doves, politicians and playboys, liberals as well as conservatives, a standard item in the arsenal of men's fashion.

More recently the warrior look invaded the runways of top designers in the form of combat and cargo pants. Camouflage patterns that span the range from the vintage British disruptive pattern to the tiger stripe used in Vietnam can be found in the couture collections of Versace and the aisles of Marks & Spencer.

According to Martin, "Military dress is paradoxically both the embodiment of heroes—in an Eisenhower jacket or Napoleonic tailoring—and the combat-ready usefulness of clothing, a merger of the real and epic. War yields a perverse effect in becoming a socialized and beautiful ideal for dress."

When Cary Grant wore a tuxedo or a suit, it lived up to the high standards of the military uniform. Sometimes the influence was literal. Oleg Cassini said that when he met Cary Grant, in 1945, he noted that in addition to his charm, which was "a force of nature," he was "wearing a striped regimental tie with his white shirt and blue blazer."

During the filming of *An Affair to Remember*, Grant halted production because the buttons on the

OVERLEAF LEFT:
CG in the South of France for the filming of To Catch a Thief *(1955). "Everything about Cary was stamped 'original,'" remarked producer Robert Evans. "Fashion is temporary. Style lasts forever."*

OVERLEAF RIGHT:
CG on the set of The Philadelphia Story *(1941). "When you say 'movie star' Cary Grant epitomizes that persona. It fit him."*
—Martin Landau

uniforms of the stewards aboard the *Queen Mary* were incorrect. The producers tried to appease him by saying that no one would notice or care. But *he* would notice, *he* would care. Uniforms were not trivial things to him. To defy their aesthetic value would be somewhat akin to desecrating the flag; well, almost.

For this behavior he was sometimes called a fusspot, a temperamental titan (though ultimately a lovable one), but as Charles Eames, whose mid-century modern furniture pieces are now considered works of art, once said, "The details are not the details. They make the design."

Robert Wolders, who was married to actress Merle Oberon and after her death lived with Audrey Hepburn for the last eleven years of her life says,

"Having known a few elegant people, I think in all of them their personal style is a result of their unwillingness to compromise on their values and their ability to focus on what's basic and real. And that applies to their choice of garment, as well, because invariably in achieving the way they look, they show a good deal of stubbornness; they know what they want, and they're likely to resist fashion, outside influences. It's the sense they develop of appropriateness and decorum. But it's always mixed with a sense of irony and humor. They take themselves seriously but not too seriously. Otherwise they become stuffy."

There's a reason why every girl loves a man in uniform. Just ask Mae West. When she spotted Cary Grant in his naval uniform on the Paramount lot that day, she saw more than just a handsome man who stood out among a crowd of handsome men. She saw a man who was dressed to kill.

HATS OFF AND BYE-BYE TO BOW TIES

"Know, first, who you are, and then adorn yourself accordingly."

—Epictetus

Grant, pictured here on the set of To Catch a Thief, *looked good in everything—even a towel.*

Esquire magazine once said that "Cary Grant is so extraordinarily attractive that he looks good in practically anything." And it's true. Cary Grant looked good in a ponytail *(Gunga Din)*, a dress *(I Was a Male War Bride)*, a mustache *(The Last Outpost)*, and even a terry-cloth towel *(North by Northwest)*. He looked good in anything.

Almost anything.

Hats were one exception. He did *not* look good in hats.

Bow ties were another.

HATS. There was something about the shape of his fine face, the square-jawed perfection, the solid features that made a hat seem superfluous and misplaced on him, like a necktie on the statue of David. Why mess with symmetry? It was "such a nice face," as Eva Marie Saint cooed in *North by Northwest.*

It was more than just a "nice face," it was an ideal face—strong, assertive, with broad manly features and glinting dark eyes. Cary Grant needed a hat like Eric Clapton needs guitar lessons.

And he knew it.

So he seldom wore one unless he had to for a role, and these were not memorable screen moments. In Hitchcock's *Notorious* (1946), there's just one brief shot of him in a homburg. Something about the homburg just doesn't look right, and Hitchcock, seemingly aware of this, cuts away from the actor quickly to spare him any further embarrassment. Grant doesn't wear the hat; the hat seems to wear him, floating or rather hovering on his head, odd looking and awkward.

But this was an era when men wore hats, so it was hard to get away from them, at least entirely.

Unlike Humphrey Bogart and Robert Mitchum, who could make use of a hat to reveal character, a hat to Grant was just no damn good. He didn't need it. He did just fine

Grant stopped wearing hats (unless a role demanded it) at a time when they were a menswear staple because B. P. Schulberg, the head of Paramount in the 1930s, where Grant was under contract, felt that they did not suit him. Grant agreed.

pulse beat a little quicker, something that had nothing to do with his foreign policy.

Soon hats were passé, thanks to JFK, a fusty thing of the past, a fixture of another age, like spats or suspenders. JFK had a thick head of hair. Grant had a gorgeous head of hair. Jet black and slicked back, it was always parted with surgical precision, as if grazed by an axe. His hair was the darkness that made the light in his face shine. Why ruin it with a hat, why spoil an effect splendidly created by nature?

Back in the forties hats were the thing, thanks in part to actors like Bogart and Mitchum, who paired them with a mackintosh and helped create the iconic tough-guy detective. Sam Spade or Philip Marlowe; take your pick. They'd look naked without a hat. They even wore them *indoors.* Hats were put to all kinds of handy uses on-screen. You could peer out from under them and look mysterious. You could take them off and put them on, for effect, or tip them kindly to a lady. And they gave you something to do with your hands. You could tilt them this way and that, depending on the emotional note you wished to sound. They gave an actor attitude, a prop second only to the cigarette. Hats were also ring-a-ding-ding cool. Frank Sinatra loved hats, wore them well into the 1950s and early 1960s, when they were no longer fashionable. He didn't care. In fact he made a fetish of the snap-brim model, even memorialized it in a tune called "The Way You Wear Your Hat," one of his signature songs.

Hats were just as popular in the movies of the fifties, particularly cowboy hats. But Grant didn't follow the course of his contemporaries; he didn't make any Westerns, which were at their peak and drew a guaranteed moneymaking audience. Kirk Douglas, Mitchum, Dean Martin, Jimmy Stewart, and even Sinatra found a home or two on the range. And got rich. They often produced these saddle-'em-up vehicles, further enhancing their wealth and box-office status. But Grant, fiercely independent, went his own way,

without it. He was already ahead of his time, a modern man, part of the future, the hatless era that had not yet arrived, would not arrive until the early 1960s, when JFK would sound the death knell for hats by refusing to wear one on the campaign trail. A man in public without a hat? In the sartorial sense, this was bold, very bold for its time. Downright revolutionary. But women took notice of JFK's revealing omission; a full head of hair is sexy. Either by shrewd discernment or by sheer accident, JFK grasped this. And men took notice of the women who took notice of the political heartthrob who made their

hatless but happy, setting his own stylistic standard. He produced and starred in romantic comedies—equaling if not surpassing the success of the Westerns churned out by his brethren—all tailor-made for him, and he slipped into them like he slipped into a Savile Row suit.

Grant's films of this era hold up better than any corny cowboy flick, even those starring the Chairman of the Board. Old Blue Eyes astride a horse? Sitting tall in the saddle? Not exactly how we think of him today. But *The Bachelor and the Bobby-Soxer*, *Dream Wife*, *That Touch of Mink*, *Mr. Blandings Builds His Dream House*, and *Houseboat*

allowed Grant to be his urbane and urban self, a hatless wonder with hair that shone like the best moussed-up metrosexual in Manhattan.

For Grant, of course, the suit was the thing. While his contemporaries used hats to add nuance to their characters, Grant remained capless but always resplendent, introducing a kind of sartorial minimalism to the world of style. By the late fifties the suit was his trademark, an immaculate gray suit. For Sinatra it was all about The Way You Wear Your Hat. For Grant it was all about The Way You Wear Your Suit. Not a fancy suit. Not a particularly expensive-looking suit. Just a plain gray suit. He somehow managed to make the plain gray banker's suit seem impossibly glamorous, sexy, elegant, even daring. The shirt, flawless white, the tie, knotted with surgical precision, completed the look. And that was it. That was enough. His suit spoke for him, sang for him.

But it didn't stop there.

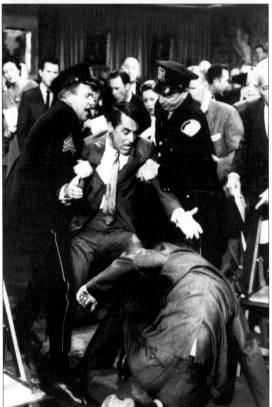

SUITS. The suit on Grant transcended itself, became as impenetrable as armor. In *North by Northwest* he is forcibly intoxicated, nearly driven off a cliff, manhandled by thugs, stuffed into the sleeper compartment of a cross-country train, shot at, and in one of the most imaginative sequences on film, chased through a cornfield by a crop duster bent on decapitating him.

Hitchcock joyfully placed Grant into the most absurd ordeals, as if toying with and teasing him, deriving a kind of sadistic enjoyment—and exquisite dramatic tension— from the established fact that here is an urbane actor perfectly dressed, immaculately attired, more suited to the drawing room than the landscape of the action hero. The joke seems to be on Grant, but only momentarily, for Grant turns the tables by remaining unruffled, his suit dusty, maybe a bit scuffed here and there, but nothing a good dry cleaner couldn't take care of in a few hours.

It's almost as if Cary Grant is equally determined to save his life *and* his suit as he perilously dangles from the presidential chins and noses carved on Mount Rushmore. The suit is the life giver, the talisman, and the amulet, the lucky charm. The suit and the man are inextricably linked. Like Samson's hair, harm one, and you harm the other.

"The spies come at you from all directions . . . Dodge a killer plane, meet a beautiful spy, don't drop your microfilm, run from the cops, killers, secret agents, beautiful women and see if you can do all this without wrinkling your suit!"
—From the movie poster for *North by Northwest*

Before the crop duster appears in the distance, Grant converses with a local yokel, a man waiting for a bus on the side of the deserted

Grant in the Hitchcock thriller North by Northwest. *Despite being roughed up by thugs (left) and chased by a crop duster (opposite), his Savile Row suits remained as crisp and functional as Superman's cape.*

highway. It's a hot day but the stranger, presumably a farmer dressed up for a big day in the city, wears a three-piece suit and broad-rimmed hat. The hot weather doesn't warrant it, but in the fifties you just didn't leave the house without a hat and a coat. It would be the contemporary equivalent of leaving home without your credit cards or cell phone. Grant, on the other hand, doesn't even seem to be carrying a pen or a wallet, for no unsightly bulges mar his trim silhouette. Not even pocket change, not even the flimsiest object to shield him from the dangerous elements, nothing with which to protect himself. Just the suit. The indestructible suit. The suit, before it becomes armor—his superhero costume—makes him seem vulnerable, naked, alone. But this is not just any suit. This is the suit of Cary Grant!

Grant knew what we know now—that knowing what *not* to wear is as important as knowing what to wear.

Was his sartorial sense impeccable? Hardly. He was—dare we say it?—mortal. He missed a few times, but this was all part of his stylistic development, and we can learn as much from his blunders as we can from his successes. The suit was his grand achievement. The bow tie was not.

BOW TIES. A bow tie on Cary Grant is like a three-piece suit on Johnny Depp, an ascot on Colin Farrell.

But Grant *loved* bow ties. At least early on. Zeppo Marx was to blame. Zeppo had always been an inspiration, so Grant caught the bow-tie bug from him and copied it. "I'd been to the Palace," Grant recalled, "to see the Marx Brothers, billed as the 'Greatest Comedy Act in Show Business, Barring None.' I noticed that

Zeppo, the young handsome one, the 'straight' man, the fellow I copied (who else?) wore a miniature, neatly tied bow tie. It was called—hold on to your chair—a jazz bow. Well, if that was the fashion, it was at least inexpensive enough for me to follow."

On Zeppo they looked sweet, but on Grant they looked silly, daft, superfluous. (Even today bow ties are best left to nerdy on-air Republican commentators like Tucker Carlson or George Will.) But Grant was feeling his way, a stranger in a strange land, trying to get a handle on a marketable look. Consequently he acquired "the corniest habits in my attempt to become quickly Americanized."

So he had to learn the hard way. By trial and error. We don't think of him as a student of style today; we think of him as the personification of style, the inventor, as if he were born with it; but that is not the case, that is the myth.

He wore a polka-dotted bow tie in the 1938 film *Holiday*, costarring Katharine Hepburn. It never seems to come to rest on his neck. Rather, it sits awry, often lopsided like a bent propeller, twisted and shapeless, as if the tie itself knows it doesn't belong on this great neck. Grant touches and teases it, straightens it, tries his best to use it to maximum comic effect but never quite pulls it off. Finally the actress who plays Hepburn's sister in the film says what the audience is already thinking, "Please change that awful tie."

And so Grant said bye-bye to bow ties, and they were seldom seen anywhere near his person again.

He had to learn through experimentation and even embarrassment, just like the rest of us. But developing a personal style, he discovered, is worth a grown man's time.

Grant wore a bow tie in a few pictures, including Holiday, *with Katharine Hepburn, but rarely offscreen. The traditional necktie was far more flattering to the shape and proportion of his face, and he knew it.*

TWO

THE AWFUL TRUTH

"Style is knowing who you are, what you want to say and not giving a damn."—GORE VIDAL

CARY GRANT was not bisexual. Cary Grant was not a homosexual. Cary Grant was a man of style.

But any man who practiced the fine art of personal style back then was called something else. As Jack Nicholson once said, "When they say you're a faggot, that's when you know you're a star."

And after the release of *I'm No Angel* (1933), the follow-up to the hit *She Done Him Wrong*, Cary Grant was an even bigger star.

But stardom had taken him by surprise. Audiences were so spellbound by his good looks and the reflected glamour of glittery Mae West that they didn't notice his awkward acting. They mistook his suppressed nervousness for a kind of macho aloofness. Even the studio itself didn't know quite what to do with him. He was cast in a series of forgettable films, including *Alice in Wonderland* (1933) and *Enter Madame* (1935).

Grant handled rumors that he'd had a carnal relationship with fellow actor Randolph Scott (above) with patience, intelligence, and most of all, a sharp wit. "When I was a young and popular star," Grant told Peter Bogdanovich, "I'd meet a girl with a man and maybe she'd say something nice about me and then the guy would say, 'Yeah, but I hear he's really a fag.' It's ridiculous, but they say it about all of us. Now in fact, that guy is doing me a favor. Number one, he's expressed an insecurity about the girl. Number two, he has provoked curiosity about me in her. Number three, that girl zeroes in on my bed to see for herself, and the result is that the guy has created the exact situation he wanted to avoid."

After he left Paramount, in 1936, he found himself in demand, but the pictures weren't any more distinguished. He received glowing reviews that same year for his brisk, off-beat portrayal of a crooked cockney in *Sylvia Scarlett*, but the movie was a commercial failure and incited the American Association of Theatre Owners to label its star, Katharine Hepburn, "box-office poison."

Then he was loaned out to RKO for a series of pictures in which he slipped into yet another "uniform," one that would eventually become his sartorial trademark. But *When You're in Love* and *The Toast of New York* were snidely called "tuxedo romances," fluffy comedies in which he was more mannequin than movie star.

The Cary Grant persona was still quite rough around the edges—and no one knew it better than he did.

"I cultivated raising one eyebrow, and tried to imitate those who put their hands in their pockets with a certain amount of ease and nonchalance," he recalled years later. "But at times, when I put my hand in my trouser pocket with what I imagined was great elegance, I couldn't get the blinking thing out again because it dripped from nervous perspiration!"

Where was Lee Strasberg when he needed him? Konstantin Stanislavski? Gilbert Adrian, Edith Head? Or for that matter Ralph Lauren, who later became his friend and whose distinguished duds helped Robert Redford confidently shine in *The Great Gatsby* (1974), or menswear designer Alan Flusser, whose silky threads gave Michael Douglas's Oscar-winning portrayal of greedy Gordon Gekko in *Wall Street* (1987) a memorably evil pinstriped panache? Some of them weren't even born yet.

"The male movie stars of that era didn't have the luxury of big wardrobe departments and stylists swirling around them," says Carlo Brandelli, creative director of Kilgour, the Savile Row tailors who supplied Grant's elegant fourteen-gauge mid-gray worsted-wool suits

"He had such fun in performing. He was so full of joy. You could see it in his body. You could see it in his face. He just let it all out."
—Eva Marie Saint

for *North by Northwest*, among other films. "The movie stars would use their own wardrobes. They were film stars *because* they were also incredibly elegant men. Their wardrobe just went hand in hand with the work they did, so they'd obviously be at their tailors. It would be Cary Grant going to his tailors, putting something together, hoping to produce a suitable look."

In other words he was more or less on his own.

According to close friend and author Roderick Mann, "he was a work in progress. Hollywood gave him the name, but he was the one who would transform himself."

He couldn't go on playing Mae West's boy toy forever, the object of lines such as, "Is that a gun in your pocket, or are you just glad to see me?"

Tall, dark, and handsome only got you so far in Hollywood. If he wanted to become a commanding leading man with the stature of a Gary Cooper or Clark Gable, able to pick and choose his own projects, then he would have to evolve—but evolve into what? That was the difficult question. His next move was a critical one; his career would depend on it.

HE NEEDN'T have worried (although of course he did), for the process was already in motion, begun decades earlier in the days of an Edwardian childhood.

Although his parents were poor, barely able to manage, in his words, "a presentable existence," they scraped together enough money to arrange piano lessons for him.

His mother, Elsie, was particularly determined to make sure he had the opportunities for a better life. When Archie was four and a half years old, she badgered the headmaster of the Bishop Road elementary school into admitting him a half year earlier than the customary age of five because her son, you see, was a bright and talented tot and, therefore, worthy of special treatment.

In rigidly class-structured England, a boy born without "airs and graces" often wound up like his father, working in a menial job during the day and haunting the local pubs at night. But Elsie would make sure her son did not go down that road.

"Cary Grant, whose previous work has too often been that of a charm merchant, turns actor in the role of the unpleasant Cockney and is surprisingly good at it."

— FROM A *NEW YORK TIMES* REVIEW OF *SYLVIA SCARLETT* STARRING CARY GRANT AND KATHARINE HEPBURN

Despite their impoverishment, and in defiance of the rigid strictures of a class-structured society, she would instill in him a sense of possibility.

And nowhere were her hopes and dreams for her young son more poignantly expressed than in the way she dressed him—not in the limp linen collars that were commonly worn by other boys in his peer group but, rather, in the smarter Eton collars made of stiff celluloid. They were costly, painfully so because money was scarce, but they were distinctive, and that was what mattered.

And when it came time for him to graduate from little-boy shorts to grown-up long pants and Mrs. Leach couldn't afford the cost of this new addition to his wardrobe, she made the pants herself. It was, in effect, his first bespoke garment, and he supervised every detail of it.

Now nine years old, he was already evincing a precocious sense of style. He insisted on not just any trousers. They had to be white flannel, which was quite a fashion statement for a young lad in the drab year of 1913.

But it wasn't stylishness for its own sake; it had an express purpose. He'd fallen in love with a girl, the butcher's daughter, and he depended on the smart attire to give him the confidence to woo her.

This first clothing collaboration was not a success. "Those homemade trousers," he remembered ruefully, "didn't seem to fit or appear as well, nor was the flannel of the same quality as the shop-bought, ready-made version of white flannels I saw on other boys. I was crestfallen. The long hours of my mother's labor and love went unappreciated, until now as I look back on it. How sad that we can't know what we know until we know it. I wonder if the appearance of my name on so many best-dressed lists is a consequence of the boyish shame from wearing those homemade flannel trousers."

As frustrating as the experience might have been for Elsie, she wasn't about to give up on her son. If he could not be a titled duke or an earl with inherited wealth and vast land holdings, then he could still be a gentleman. Elsie insisted he respectfully raise his cap and speak politely to his elders as well as polish his shoes and keep his clothes spotlessly clean. She would extract two pence from his modest allowance for each stain he made on the white linen tablecloth on which family dinners were served. He was, you might say, a man of style in training: well dressed, well groomed, and well mannered.

They were qualities that would not only be the roots of his future persona but,

"Permit me to suggest that you dress neatly and cleanly. A young person who dresses well usually behaves well. Good manners and a pleasant personality, even without a college education, will take you far." —CG

he believed, an integral part of his future success, not only as a movie star but as a person. "Permit me to suggest that you dress neatly and cleanly," he counseled in 1962, at the age of fifty-eight, when he was making *Charade* with Audrey Hepburn. "A young person who dresses well usually behaves well. Good manners and a pleasant personality, even without a college education, will take you far."

Corny advice by today's standards, perhaps, not the kind of thing you'd hear from hard-charging motivational speakers like Tony Robbins or Suze Orman, but it worked wonderfully well for the gentle and modest Archie Leach.

He made a lasting impression not only on the movie industry but on the people he met, even in the most casual of circumstances, by personifying these simple and what we might cynically call "quaint" virtues.

Cosmopolitan magazine editor Helen Gurley Brown, who sat next to him at an American Film Institute luncheon, recalled that he was so much fun she didn't even notice what he was wearing.

"He was a big star, larger than life," she recalls, "and he knew it. He knew, too, that the person he was about to meet might be intimidated by that, so he immediately set about putting you at ease. We gossiped throughout the entire luncheon, and before long it felt more like I was chatting with an old friend than a legend."

Rob Wolders, married at the time to the glamorous actress Merle Oberon, recalls a similar experience, but this one took place in his kitchen.

"I remember very clearly the first time I met him," says Wolders. He continues: "Merle and I were living in Malibu. One day I came home from the city about four o'clock in the afternoon, and I walked into the kitchen and there were

CG in a stand-out tie in a stand-out movie, 1937's The Awful Truth, *which made him an A-list actor. More than forty years later his fondness for polka-dot ties would inspire Beverly Hills fashion designer Amir to make him similar ties in silk, voile, and mixed-fiber fabrics.*

Merle, Larry Olivier, and Cary Grant making tea. I'd never met either of the two men. Olivier was at the stove boiling the water. We had no staff in the house. And they stayed in the kitchen, which shows the coziness of the situation. And the conversation was about their children. Grant had taken a house on the beach because he and Dyan Cannon were in the midst of a difficult divorce, and he wanted to be close to the baby, Jennifer; and Olivier had rented William Wyler's house, which was just three or four houses away, and the three had been walking along the beach and had run into each other.

"Cary immediately put me at ease. Olivier was nice, but a little bit stand-offish, a bit chilly, but Cary was full of fun and knew how to bring you into the conversation without it ever seeming forced. I think it was because he was genuinely interested in people. I think that was the secret to his charm. It was a lovely experience I must say."

To Beverly Hills fashion designer Amir, who designed shirts and ties for Grant in his later years, some with the white polka dots against a black background similar to the kind he wears in *The Awful Truth*, he was more than charming: he was an inspiration, even to this day.

"He inspires me," says Amir, "to do the best in everything I do. The secret to his charm was that he was a good listener as well as a good talker. He was genuinely interested in you. You could meet him the next day or the next year, and he would still remember the little things about you."

Elsie Leach had indeed raised "a proper little gentleman," but he was by no means a priss. He was as boisterous, rebellious, and restless as any of the lads he joined in the school yard for football and other games; at times he was downright wicked. "The worst thing I ever did as a child," he confessed, "and it was dreadful, was to set fire to a little girl's dress with a match. She ran off screaming to her mother, who put her out!"

His fun-loving father, whom he described as "sporty-looking," only added fuel to the conflagration. Elias Leach liked to knock back a few pints and belt out popular English music-hall songs like "The Man Who Broke the Bank at Monte Carlo." He'd invite his son to join along, raising quite a ruckus, to the chagrin of the prim and proper Elsie.

Elsie took Archie to the more genteel movie houses of the day like the Claire Street Cinema, which served tea during the shows. Elias, on the other hand, took him to the rowdy Metropole, a drafty barnlike building that was full of manly smells like tobacco smoke and wet raincoats.

Before the show Archie and his father often stopped off at tuckshops to buy bars of chocolate or peppermint candy, which they ate while watching Archie's idols Charlie Chaplin, Mack Swain, and "Bronco Billy" Anderson, the cowboy star.

Away from the critical eye of Mrs. Leach, Archie and his father cut loose, roaring with laughter at the slapstick antics of the great comedians of the day. The place shook with the knee slapping and foot stomping of the caterwauling crowd. "I thought what a *marvelous* place," Grant recalled.

THE ENTERTAINMENT industry was booming then, even in the provinces. In 1912 there were more than three and a half thousand cinemas in England, most of them packed to the rafters during weekend matinees. Archie saw a vast variety of entertainment—music-hall acts, pantomimes, comedians, acrobats, short films, serials, and magic tricks. He loved them all, especially the serials. *The Clutching Hand*, which starred Pearl White, a dishy damsel who enflamed his adolescent lust, was his favorite.

It's no wonder he preferred going to the cinema with his father. "We lived and loved each adventure," he said of these outings with Elias, "and each following week I neglected a lot of school homework conjecturing how that hero and heroine could possibly get out of the extraordinary fix in which they'd been left."

Elias Leach was not surprisingly Grant's first style model. "I often sat fascinated," he recalled, "at the way my father kept his stylish mustache from drowning in the teacup as he drank."

Archie also picked up sound sartorial tips from his dad, a pants presser at Todd's, a large clothing manufacturer in England. His father advised him to purchase "one good superior suit rather than a number of inferior ones" because "even when it is threadbare, people will know it was once good."

Later in life, when Archie Leach became Cary Grant, consistently praised as one of the best-dressed men in the world, he never deviated from this sartorial philosophy. His wardrobe remained relatively sparse for a man of his considerable wealth, filled with only the highest-quality suits and shoes, many custom made to his exact specifications.

Although his father was influential in the formulation of what would eventually be his unique style, the *coup de foudre*—the bolt of lightning—didn't strike until 1920, when at the age of sixteen and a member of the traveling Pender troupe, he met Hollywood's greatest sword-swinging adventurer, Douglas Fairbanks Sr., on board the S.S. *Olympic*, bound for America. Grant recalled the incident in an autobiographical magazine article in 1963: "Among the fellow passengers were newlyweds Douglas Fairbanks Sr. and Mary Pickford, the world's most popular honeymooners and the first film stars I ever met. They were gracious and patient in face of constant harassment, by people with cameras and autograph books, whenever they appeared on deck; and once even I found myself being photographed with Mr. Fairbanks during a game of shuffleboard. As I stood beside him I tried with shy, inadequate words to tell him of my adulation. He was a splendidly trained athlete and acrobat, affable and warmed by success and well-being. A gentleman in the true sense of the word. A gentle man. Only a strong man can be gentle; and it suddenly dawns on me that I've doggedly striven to keep tanned ever since, only because of a desire to emulate his healthful appearance."

Many of the layers of Grant's personal style derive from this seminal meeting: the athletic attention to health and fitness, the gracious manners, the sporty but stylish air, even the tan—and the all-important idea that style is an outward projection of the inner man.

WHEN ARCHIE'S MOTHER had "vanished," secretly shuttled off to a sanatorium, and things at home fell apart, Archie lived with "a void in my life, a sadness of spirit that affected each daily activity with which I occupied myself in order to overcome it."

His father spent his time struggling to support a second family and wasn't around to console his son; those jolly visits to the cinema were less frequent. Archie, as a result, suffered a kind of second abandonment while he was still in the throes of the first. Although he described Elias Leach as a "handsome man" with a "fancy moustache," he viewed his father's outwardly cheerful disposition as a cover for the "sad acceptance of the dull life he had chosen."

Archie's backstage job at the Empire Theatre as an electrician's assistant provided a much-welcomed diversion from the turbulence and gloom at home; it also gave him his first glimpse of the inner workings of his future profession.

He was thirteen and awestruck by the "dazzling land of smiling, jostling people wearing and not wearing all sorts of costumes and doing all sorts of clever things." After that there was no doubt in his mind about his future profession. "And that's when I knew! But an actor's life for me!"

By the time he boarded the *Olympic*, in July of 1920, he was a young but proficient member of Bob Pender's team of comic acrobats, enjoying his newfound craft. The paternal Pender had trained him and given him a job, "a place to be," but the meeting with Fairbanks did something much more. Purely by his stylish example, Fairbanks showed him that life did not have to be a relentlessly dreary affair, that it wasn't all a vale of tears. Life could also be a celebration.

From that day on he would shrewdly select the qualities of the people he admired, beginning a transformation that would last a lifetime.

Fortunately for him there was no dearth of exemplary figures to model himself after, so by the time he walked onto the set of *The Awful Truth* in 1937, his hand no longer got stuck in his pocket soppy with sweat. He had mastered the quality of studied nonchalance that had previously eluded him. The days of ill-fitting white flannels were also long behind him. He was now well into his Savile Row period. He knew by then not only what flattered his physique but what didn't. He had arrived at a thorough understanding of the technical details of tailoring—how, for instance, to adjust a garment to further enhance its visual appeal. The custom-made Hawes & Curtis suits are his own, cut to accentuate his sleek silhouette and downplay his less flattering attributes.

He learned not only by working closely with his tailors but also by careful observation of the stars he worked with at Paramount. Marlene Dietrich and Mae West were particularly skillful in this area. Mae West, for instance, had designer Travis Banton make her two versions of the same dress: one formfittingly tight to stand in and another she could sit down in without busting a seam.

He also mastered the tricky business of mixing patterns, a lost art. A polka-dot tie—much like the ones Amir would make for him decades later—jazzed up a dark pinstriped double-breasted jacket in *The Awful Truth*, a madcap comedy about a divorce that hinges on who gets custody of the couple's dog.

The swashbuckling Douglas Fairbanks Sr. was one of Grant's early idols. They met aboard the S.S. Olympic in 1920 when Grant, sixteen, was on his way to America as a member of an acrobatic troupe.

"He was a splendidly trained athlete and acrobat, affable and warmed by success and well-being," recalled Grant years later. "A gentleman in the true sense of the word. A gentle man. Only a strong man can be gentle."

In the scene in which he says to Irene Dunne, "Nothing can happen to me now," just as the piano lid suddenly closes on his hand, he's wearing a pinstriped three-piece suit with a striped shirt and a checked tie; the patterns blend harmoniously, a feat he learned from observing the ultimate man of 1930s style, the Duke of Windsor, whom Oleg Cassini called "the best dressed man I ever saw."

Although Grant is remembered for his stubbornly conservative look, it wasn't always that way. In *The Awful Truth*, as a young man of thirty-three, he appears downright trendy, wearing jackets with smart wide lapels, espe-

cially compared to the boxy tweeds worn by his costar Ralph Bellamy. He also sports a fancier Spitalsfield instead of the tamer-patterned Macclesfield tie. Both Spitalsfield and Macclesfield ties were wardrobe staples of the best-dressed men of the era, including socialite Anthony J. Drexel Biddle and Baron Nicolas de Gunzberg.

But what elevated Grant from a mere fashion plate was the emergence of his trademark wit, a trait he developed by observing Noel Coward at dinner parties in the 1920s. Although he might have been nervous on the inside, unsure of director Leo McCarey's improvisational and often chaotic approach to film-making, Grant was at least outwardly relaxed and confident enough to ad lib some of the film's funniest lines. When he unexpectedly turns up at the apartment he once shared with wife Irene Dunne, who asks him why he's come back, he replies because "the judge says it's my day to see the dog."

> *By the time he walked onto the set of* The Awful Truth *in 1937, his hand no longer got stuck in his pocket . . . . He had mastered the quality of studied non-chalance that had previously eluded him. The days of ill-fitting white flannels were also long behind him. He was now well into his Savile Row period.*

The Awful Truth, which one critic called "a comedy of *re*marriage," launched Grant into superstardom and was the first successful film to treat divorce humorously, amusing audiences with the novel idea that marriage—and divorce—could be light and funny as well as painfully sad.

Grant emerges here as a new kind of leading man. "In the films of the 1930s," says Peter Bogdanovich, "it was very unusual for a romantic lead to do what was considered comedy relief—especially physical comedy."

Grant manages to remain devilishly dashing even in the silliest slapstick scenes. He reveals his unusual graceful athleticism when he trips over the threshold of a doorway and somersaults into a wall or, in another scene, when he falls backward off a chair.

He achieves the impossible; he makes clumsiness seem elegant. (Do not try this at home.)

Outwardly unruffled—his suits never lose their flawless drape—Grant's expressions show a contrastingly inward befuddlement, a blend of disparate elements no other actor could embody with quite the same stylish aplomb.

CARY GRANT was keenly aware of the power of an elegant image as a means of promoting himself in the world, but he was so much more than a mere "charm merchant," as one reviewer put it.

As we shall see, the people he shrewdly chose to emulate were some of the most formidable figures of the nineteenth century. They came from all walks of life, from royalty and high society, industry and finance, as well as from the worlds of literature and show business.

Grant was often unfairly called "a fusspot," "a perfectionist," a neurotic who made a fetish of fastidiousness, on and off the set, but the dashing men he emulated were far more exacting than he would ever be, with resources and standards that were skyscraper high. How could a poor boy from the English provinces ever measure up, much less surpass them?

THE AWFUL
TRUTH

A Tale of Two (Or Maybe Three) Jackets

"Style that shows is only decoration, not style."

—Sidney Lumet

THE EVOLUTION OF A SIGNATURE GESTURE. *Grant in the early 1930s with his hand awkwardly thrust in the pocket of an unaccommodating "sack suit."*

Clothes do not make the man; the *right* clothes make the man. Had it not been for the right jacket, there might not have been a Cary Grant.

"He was very stiff," said Betsy Drake, Grant's third wife, about her former husband's early acting efforts. "He said you notice how my hand is in my pocket because I didn't know what to do with my hands." He himself admitted as much and added, famously, that his hand was so wet with nervous perspiration he sometimes couldn't "get the blinking thing out again."

Although inexperience and nerves were part of the problem, the wrong jacket might have been the real culprit.

Between World War I and World War II, when Grant was beginning his career, starring in films like *She Done Him Wrong* in 1932 with Mae West, the majority of well-tailored Savile Row suits were nonvented. In other words they didn't have slits. They were called sack suits, a term that aptly describes the way they fit a man's body.

Although ventless jackets hugged the hips and flattered the figure with a clean line, they functioned poorly. When the wearer slipped his hands into his trouser pockets, the ventless jacket rose up on the hip, rippling in a tidal wave of creases and cloth.

In *The Amazing Quest of Ernest Bliss* (1936), the perils of the wrong jacket are plainly on view. Grant plays a rich but depressed playboy who seeks a cure from a doctor in London's posh Harley Street. Dressed in a smart three-piece suit, he walks into the doctor's office with his hand awkwardly thrust into his pants pocket, creating a mass of distracting folds and wrinkled cloth, a gesture that jars with the suave toff he's trying to portray and the man of style he would eventually become.

The single-vented suit was another option, but it wasn't much of an improvement. The single vent appears in the rear and was designed to allow the tails of a jacket to fall naturally on each side of a cavalry man's legs when he was astride a horse.

But in its civilian incarnation, it didn't function quite as well. According to menswear designer Alan Flusser, "If a man's hand is in search of a jacket or trouser pocket, at the slightest tug the single vent pulls open like a garage door, revealing what it should be covering. This center slit attracts undue attention to the man's exposed derrière, and if cut high enough, the vent encourages a fringe of disordered shirt to join the spectacle."

These stills of Grant are from an RKO wardrobe test for the Hitchcock classic *Notorious*. Wearing a rear-vented pinstriped suit, Grant

Grant practices the gesture in a wardrobe test for 1946's Notorious *(above) and perfects it in 1959's* North by Northwest *with Eva Marie Saint (overleaf).*

experiments with a gesture that would become his trademark. From the expression on his face and the way the jacket functions, he's not completely satisfied.

It would not be until the advent of the double-vented jacket that the problem would be completely solved.

"Side vents offer the wearer the highest union of function and form," explains Flusser, "not to mention flexibility. As for function, when the wearer is sitting down, the side slit allows its back flap to move away, thereby minimizing creasing. And when one accesses a trouser pocket, the double vent's back flap permits smooth entry while concealing the buttocks."

37

To further improve the functionality of his suit jackets, Grant had his tailor lengthen the vents beyond their normal boundaries.

It's likely that he customized his single-vented as well as his double-vented suits in much the same way. This not only made the jackets more functional, but it also created the flattering illusion of greater height and slimness by leading the viewer's eye up either side of the coat's back. When Grant moves—or runs or stumbles or falls, as he does in *To Catch a Thief, North by Northwest,* and *Charade*—the suit moves gracefully with him.

With customized vents, he could make the simple gesture of putting his hands in his pocket look impossibly elegant instead of painfully awkward, as he demonstrates in this photo taken on the set of *North by Northwest* with Eva Marie Saint.

Grant had learned early on from his more experienced costars that clothes could either help or hinder a performance. Mae West had instructed designer Travis Banton to make her two versions of the same dress: one torturously tight to show off her luscious curves and one she could comfortably sit down in without splitting the seams.

Grant's wardrobe modifications helped him to achieve an enviable nonchalance and confidence. He made the ordinary gesture of putting one's hand in one's pockets seem somehow extraordinary. Mae West's success in this area seems less certain. Her figure-hugging gowns caused *Variety* to remark that she "makes interesting movements in a seated position."

THREE

STUDENT
OF STYLE

*"One pretends to do something, or copy someone
or some teacher, until it can be done confidently
and easily in what becomes one's own manner."*

— CG

DECADES AFTER meeting swashbuckling film star Douglas Fairbanks Sr. aboard the New York–bound *Olympic*, Grant would approach Ralph Lauren with a special request.

"Cary tried to convince me to make a double-breasted tuxedo like the one worn by Fairbanks," recalled Lauren in *A Class Apart*, a documentary about Grant, "same lapel and all."

Such was the indelible impression Fairbanks had made on the sixteen-year-old even after he became Cary Grant, a full-fledged style idol, his name a mainstay on international best-dressed lists.

And there had been other influences, many others.

"In my earlier career," Grant recalled, "I patterned myself on a combination of Englishmen—A. E. Matthews, Noel Coward, and Jack

CG in killer Kilgour: nobody wore pinstripes with more panache.

Buchanan, who impressed me as a character actor. He always looked so natural. I tried to copy men I thought were sophisticated and well dressed like Douglas Fairbanks or Cole Porter. And Freddie Lonsdale, the British playwright, always had an engaging answer for everything."

Grant chose his models well. These were men for whom style was more than just a sideline; it was a way of being, and sometimes, particularly in the case of A. E. Matthews, the popular British actor of the 1940s, it was a matter of life and death. When he was ninety Matthews made headlines by sitting in protest for several days and nights on the cold sidewalk outside his Georgian home in England, risking pneumonia. He was trying to prevent the city council from installing a streetlight whose design he deemed ugly.

Jack Buchanan, the dry, debonair Scottish song-and-dance man, was at the height of his popularity in the 1920s, when Grant was just beginning to develop his own debonair persona. Grant learned from Buchanan the art of mixing patterns, namely how to balance pinstripes with paisleys, checks with pin dots, for what Alan Flusser calls that extra "nuance of nattiness."

It's a skill that has been revived today by such men as musician and actor André 3000 Benjamin, who topped *Vanity Fair*'s 2005 International Best-Dressed List. "I love contrasting patterns/colors," Benjamin told *Vanity Fair*, "and wearing pocket squares gives me another chance to freak it just when you thought the ensemble was perfect. Slight imperfections or, better yet, human touches are always the move. Besides, there's a pocket there—stuff it."

> *"Originality is nothing but judicious imitation."*
> — Voltaire

In his day Buchanan certainly knew how to "freak it." He was said to own more than three hundred silk pocket hankies and enjoyed tinkering with them the way some men tinker with their golf swing.

Grant would become a man after his own heart, evidenced when he proudly announced to *Esquire* magazine in 1960 that he had originated the square-style breast pocket handkerchief.

Buchanan, a sartorial trendsetter, was one of the first to wear the tab collar, which became popular in the 1920s and 1930s and resurfaced again in the 1960s on doo-wop musicians, Teddy Boys, and other slim-suited entertainers.

In 1925 Buchanan sported a new style of trousers that were baggy enough to make the flyest rapper look twice with envy. Pleated and as roomy as pajamas, they were called Oxford bags, an innovation created by undergraduates at Oxford and Cambridge universities. They were all the rage on both continents for about a year, the precursor to the fuller-cut pants worn by today's hippest hip-hoppers.

To be called a "Buchanan" was the highest praise a man of style could receive, akin to being singled out as a Beau Brummel. But like Fred Astaire's, Buchanan's clothes had to be functional as well as fashionable, able to enhance rather than inhibit his physically demanding performances. He perfected the art of looking dapper while dancing so well that the *New York Times* in a review of one of his films called him a hoofer with "the staggering self-assurance that could turn a leaky rowboat into the *Ile de France*."

> *"He has found his style, when he cannot do otherwise."*
>
> — PAUL KLEE

It was a quality Grant would have to master himself, for the movies he made in the 1930s and 1940s—such as *Topper*, with Constance Bennett; *Holiday*, with Katharine Hepburn; and *His Girl Friday*, with Rosalind Russell—required him to perform slapstick while retaining a stylish romantic presence, no easy feat, and something no actor had achieved before and no actor has rivaled since.

In *Holiday* he performs no fewer than three stunts, all with a proficiency that would have made Bob Pender proud. He plays Johnny Case, a rube with a touchingly sincere personality who falls in love with a rich socialite. When his relatives express doubts about what is a shockingly sudden development, he tells them not to worry. "When things get tough," he says, "when I feel a worry coming on, you know what I do?" He then executes a perfect cartwheel, smiles, and concludes, "There! And then the worries are over!"

In another scene he lifts Katharine Hepburn onto his shoulders, and they launch blithely into a forward circus roll. Later Hepburn asks him, "Can you do a back flip-flop?" He says of course he can, but the story moves along before he can make good on his claim. Later he performs one. It's as exuberant and as athletically impressive as the end-zone gymnastics performed by today's NFL showboaters after they've scored a touchdown. The difference, of course, is that football players have the benefit of customized athletic gear; Grant does his stunts in a Savile Row three-piece suit.

"Only Fred Astaire ever moved as well as Cary Grant," observed David Thomson in his book *Movie Man*, "but Grant moved with more dramatic eloquence while Astaire cherished the purity of movement. Grant could look as elegant as Astaire, but he could manage to look clumsy without actually sacrificing balance or style."

Grant's fame allowed him to get to know these talented men not only as a fan but as a friend and to observe them up close as well as from afar. Freddie Lonsdale spent most of World War II in America, part of the time as Grant's houseguest. Grant called him "maddening but irresistible," and they remained close friends right up until Lonsdale's death, in 1954.

Lonsdale, like Grant, was of working-class origins, a self-made man who had consciously eradicated his Cockney accent and adopted one that was posh and polished enough to fool an Eton don.

According to Betsy Drake, "In Cary's day you got nowhere—nowhere—with a lower-class accent and he was not about to be nothing."

> *"Cary had a sense of joy—about the world, about himself. He could inspire the moment with great pleasure and fun and appreciation of life."*
> — FAY WRAY

Grant would follow Lonsdale's example, but with altogether different results. Harder edges were added to Grant's lilting West Country accent, typical of the turn-of-the-century Bristolian, as a result of the Cockney influences he picked up while working with rough-and-tumble vaudevillians. When he arrived in New York, he would consciously alter his accent to sound more aristocratic in the hope of landing the sophisticated drawing-room roles on Broadway, but it would be colored again by American speech patterns, which he loved, particularly the pitter-patter he heard at baseball games from players, umpires, and boisterous fans.

"If you listen to the way he pronounces *can't*," says Bogdanovich, "he pronounces it the way Americans do, with a hard *c*. Not the softer English way. He was definitely trying to sound American at times."

The New York Giants baseball team traveled the same circuit as the Pender troupe in the 1920s, and Grant spent much of his free time watching them compete. At first baseball seemed like a screwy version of cricket, which he'd played in England, but he grew to love America's favorite pastime and became an avid fan. In 1981, when he married his fifth wife, Barbara Harris, part of their wedding celebration included taking in a night game at Dodger Stadium, where they ate hot dogs and cheered for the home team.

The clipped part of his famous "Judy, Judy, Judy" accent derives as much from "batter up, batter up, batter up" as it does from his goal to sound like an upper-class English gent at a time when Anglomania reigned in America.

(In fact, Grant never actually said "Judy, Judy, Judy" on-screen, though imitators forever put these words in his mouth. Still, it was indicative of the cadence

of his speech pattern. Peter Bogdanovich once suggested to Grant that his frequent utterance of a single "Judy" in *Only Angels Have Wings* (in which Rita Hayworth was the Judy in question) gave rise to the famous misquote. Grant replied that he thought this a likely source.)

The variety of linguistic influences the peripatetic Grant encountered resulted in a decidedly unique and wonderfully odd manner of speaking.

"Nobody talked like Cary Grant," says Bogdanovich. "President Kennedy used to call him up just to hear him talk. Bobby, his brother the attorney general, would be on the extension. They both got a huge kick out of hearing Cary talk."

NOEL COWARD'S influence was even closer to the bone. Grant not only aspired to his glamour and sophistication, but he was professionally obligated to *become* him. In 1928, at just twenty-four years old, Grant joined the cast of the American version of the Broadway musical *Polly* and was given the role Noel

For a lifelong baseball fan like Cary Grant, one of the highlights of making That Touch of Mink *in 1962 with Doris Day was meeting Mickey Mantle, Roger Maris, and Yogi Berra in the New York Yankees dugout.*

*"I suddenly became aware that I wasn't sure what or
who I was on the screen. As an actor I had a thin veneer
of sophistication, carefully copied from Noel Coward."*

—CG

Grant learned early on from people like Noel Coward (opposite) that personal style could be a commercial commodity in itself. Pre-Hollywood Archie Leach (right), before the name change, in an ad for J. S. Beck Shoes that appeared in a New York newspaper in October 1929. Noel Coward advertising Bulova watches (below).

Coward had originated in the London production. It was only Grant's second musical comedy, and his affected nonchalance and posh pretensions were a poor parody of Coward's. And everybody noticed it: audiences as well as critics, players as well as producers.

"In the late 1920s," Grant admitted, "I wavered between imitating two older English actors of the natural, relaxed school, Sir Gerald DuMaurier and A. E. Matthews . . . but Noel Coward's performance in *Private Lives* narrowed the field, and many a musical-comedy road company was afflicted with my breezy new gestures and puzzling accent."

Polly received mainly negative reviews, and although Grant was jettisoned from the show, Coward continued to loom large as a model for his inchoate persona.

Although Coward, the son of a failed piano salesman, came from a working-class family, he wrote about rich people with such wit and insight that the public assumed he was part of that milieu. But like Lonsdale, he was a product of pure self-creation, and clothes were as much a part of it as was his literary talent.

Coward claimed that his habit of wearing flamboyant silk dressing gowns was purely functional, "wonderful things to play in because they're so comfortable to act in." Nevertheless, they caused quite a stir, and he welcomed, if not courted, the publicity. They weren't so much regarded as femi-

ARCHIE LEACH, leading man in "A Wonderful Night" says "Make every day a wonderful

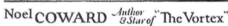

Noel COWARD *Author & Star of* "The Vortex"

NOEL COWARD *says:*
"I have learned the economy and practicability of wearing a strap watch. And I have learned that *this one* — my Bulova Watch — is every bit as accurate as it is practical."

You will find BULOVA watches at jewelers everywhere

nine as they were subversively antimasculine. Still, he persisted in flouncing about in them during interviews until they became his trademark, a symbol of the new Jazz Age—loose, smart, and glittery. He was as well known for the way he dressed as for his literary successes and stage performances. "I took to wearing coloured turtle-necked jerseys," he said, "more for comfort than effect, and soon I was informed by my evening paper that I had started a fashion."

Cecil Beaton noted that "all sorts of men suddenly wanted to look like Noel Coward—sleek and satiny, clipped and well groomed, with a cigarette, a telephone, or a cocktail in hand."

Oxford aesthetes wore Coward-style turtlenecks with their flannel bags; rugged naval captains and jaunty colonels suddenly used (and overused) the word "terribly," copying Coward's coy dialect.

And so did Grant. Up to a point. Although Grant recognized that a signature style could be useful to his career, a commercial commodity in itself, he also understood that it must be a *personal* style, not a Xerox copy of another man's. As Richard Rodgers noted, Coward "wrote with style, sang with style, painted with style, and even smoked a cigarette with a style that belonged exclusively to him."

The style that Grant developed would also be "exclusive to him," but it would take some doing. He initially became a kind of manly Noel Coward: elegant, sophisticated, but never effeminate. There would be no yellow silk socks or satin slippers in Grant's closet (none on record, anyway), no fey flourishes with a long cigarette holder, no "inclination to ruin a correct ensemble by some flashy error of taste," as Coward put it.

Grant would infuse Coward's satiny tuxedo style with Fairbanks's testosterone-charged masculinity. When Grant moved to Hollywood, in 1932, one of the first people he called on was Douglas Fairbanks Sr., who not only remembered him but invited him to the set of his new movie, *The Thief of Bagdad*, a lavish adventure romp. The aspiring young actor stood off to the side watching in awe as his hero intrepidly performed his own stunts and revealed a remarkable physical agility, qualities Grant could well appreciate as a former acrobat, tumbler, and stilt walker.

Grant would also become good friends with Fairbanks's son, Douglas Fairbanks Jr., with whom he would star in the 1939 classic *Gunga Din*, an adventure flick very much in the Fairbanks Sr. tradition. (Grant, emu-

MEN OF STYLE: *Douglas Fairbanks Jr. and Cary Grant, two A-list actors who also made the best-dressed list.*

lating his idol, insisted on performing many of his own stunts, which resulted in bruises and backaches.)

Douglas Fairbanks Jr. followed in his father's fashionable footsteps, frequently appearing on international best-dressed lists and always happy to dispense advice on one of his favorite subjects: men's clothes. "I've always thought it unwise to *over*-plan dress," he said, "and that if the quality of what you have is good it is best not to be too deliberate. A smart old hat or suit is often better looking than a new one."

Even in the late 1970s, Grant still had many of the suits he'd worn in the 1940s, all in good condition, all lovingly preserved, all capable of being updated with the right alterations.

"Trust not," warned writer Thomas Carlyle, "the heart of that man for whom old clothes are not venerable."

But clothes were only a part of what made these men appealing role models to a fledgling entertainer eager for guidance. A sharp wit was as much a part of their style as the cut and fabric of their Savile Row suits.

Lonsdale's quips, for instance, could be as sharp as a coffin nail. He was at a New Year's Eve party in London's posh Garrick Club and was asked by actor Seymour Hicks to patch things up with a chap with whom Lonsdale had had a row. Hicks told Lonsdale that at such a time it was best to let bygones be bygones. "Go over," said Hicks, "and wish him a happy New Year." Lonsdale reluctantly crossed the room and said to his enemy, "I wish you a happy New Year. But only one."

A. E. Matthews was also quick with a quip. When he was nearly ninety, he was at a luncheon to celebrate fifty years of filmmaking at Pinewood Studios in England, during which long-winded Sir Leonard Brockington delivered a speech that seemed to go on forever. After twenty-five minutes Brockington paused, prompting guests to applaud. When the din faded, Brockington continued. Exasperated, Matthews exclaimed, "My God, doesn't he know I haven't got long to live?"

"Wit," said Noel Coward, "ought to be a glorious treat, like caviar. Never spread it about like marmalade." But he doesn't seem to have followed his own advice, for his "Noelisms," as his quips were called, are as numerous as they are amusing. During rehearsals for one of his plays, he told an actor, "If you must have motivation, think of your pay packet on Friday." After seeing David Lean's great epic, *Lawrence of Arabia*, he told its handsome young star, Peter O'Toole, that if he'd been any prettier, "it would have been *Florence of Arabia*."

During a run-through of the revue *Sigh No More*, Coward noticed that one of the actors was the victim of what we would call today a wardrobe malfunction. "For God's sake," Coward said to the show's choreographer, Wendy Toye, "go and tell that young man to take his Rockingham tea service out of his tights!"

Charles Cochran, the West End wonder who is remembered as the "British Ziegfeld" for his string of hit productions that included Noel Coward's *Private Lives*, Rogers & Hart's *Ever Green*, and Cole Porter's *Anything Goes*, also got a taste of Coward's racy side.

"Mae West told me she was working on a new play," he recalled. "I enquired what it was about and she replied. 'It's about this guy. He's a cocksucker and—.' Shocked, I made a hasty excuse and left. When I told the story to Noel Coward he said, 'I have never heard a plot begin so promisingly.'"

Although Coward and Grant eventually became close friends, each admiring the other's unique talents, raunchy humor was never Grant's cup of tea. Although he might have chuckled at Coward's jolting jibes, he developed a brand of wit that was informed by his own urbane tastes and sensibilities.

When Grant was offered the lead role in the movie *My Fair Lady*, he told the producer that not only wouldn't he accept the part, but if the role of Professor Henry Higgins wasn't given to Rex Harrison, he wouldn't even go see it. (Harrison got the part and won an Oscar for his performance.)

As Grant's fame grew it seemed every comic on earth was likely to do a Cary Grant imitation. When a reporter asked him who he thought did the best impression, Grant said, "I do."

But the important lesson Grant learned from Coward was that wit could be employed as a tool. Coward used it to generate publicity; Grant used it to deflect it. When an interviewer asked the star of *To Catch a Thief*, *Indiscreet*, and *An Affair to Remember*, "Who is Cary Grant?" he responded, "When you find out, let me know." The answer revealed his lifelong uneasiness with his dueling identities, the one he was born with and the one he invented, much like his often-quoted comment, "Everybody wants to be Cary Grant. Even *I* want to be Cary Grant."

GRANT ALSO HAD the great good fortune to have arrived in America at a time when men's fashion was at its height. In the years between World War I and World War II, decorum was a goal of the average Joe as well as the movie star and the aristocrat. Middle-class men wore suits to ball games and rolled up their French cuffs to water the lawn, and rich men respectfully addressed poor men as "Mister." Civility was the rule, not the exception.

And style in all things was valued as much as talent—or rather was viewed as a kind of talent of its own. When a radio interviewer accused novelist Michael Arlen of not being able to write as well as Evelyn Waugh, the author of *Brideshead Revisited*, Arlen responded, "Ah, yes, that's quite true; but I *dress* better than Evelyn."

Even comics had sartorial flair back then, some more than others. As a stilt-walking member of Pender's "Giants" traveling the American vaudeville circuit of the Roaring Twenties, Archie met his childhood idols the Marx Brothers. Groucho was the star, the one who got all the laughs, but it was Zeppo, the dapper straight man, who caught Archie's eye.

Archie copied Zeppo's slicked-back hairstyle, obtained by the application of brilliantine. But Archie improved it, at least for his purposes, by mixing it with Dixie Peach, the pomade used by black performers of the era, creating what we would call today the perfect "product." The hybrid goo gave his hair a sophisticated blue-black sheen that would fit right in among the mousses and gels at Frédéric Fekkai and other of today's top salons.

It might seem like a trivial addition to his personal grooming arsenal, but it advanced his image in the world by turning his boyishly tousled locks into a more grown-up coif, his first step away from the clownish vaudevillian and toward the romantic leading man he would eventually become.

This restyling, coupled with his tall athletic build, handsome features, and good manners, got him noticed, particularly by fashionable females. Although still an awkward teen in many ways, he was, as Pauline Kael wrote, "an incredible charmer," and for a time he became an escort, chaperoning such socialites as opera singer Lucrezia Bori to dinner parties, where he made the most of the experience by studying the behavior and dress of the upper classes.

Countess Dorothy di Frasso said that "he wasn't so much attracted to aristocrats as he was to the aristocratic style—the dignity of bearing, the self confidence, all the things to which he aspired."

Self-improvement for him was both a survival mechanism and a passion that lasted his entire life, even through his retirement, when he would begin the day by clipping edifying articles from newspapers and magazines to be filed away for future reference.

During these glamorous social occasions of the 1920s, he met captains of industry as well as glamorous socialites and gleaned all he could from them, everything from the intricacies of financial investing to how to light a lady's cig-

arette with seductive ease, as he does in *North by Northwest* for Eva Marie Saint after they share their first meal together in the train's dining car.

CG lights Eva Marie Saint's cigarette with panache in the Hitchcock classic North by Northwest *(1959).*

On location in Lonepine, California, for *Gunga Din*, he would rise early to monitor the world's financial markets, then engage in arbitrage, a practice at which he was particularly adept.

He also made important career contacts at these parties, such as George Tilyou, whose family owned and operated Steeplechase Park in Brooklyn's Coney Island. Tilyou hired him as a kind of stilt-walking billboard to advertise the park's racetrack. Not the most glamorous job in the world, but he was glad to have it. In fact without it, there might never have been a Cary Grant. The job paid him forty dollars a week at a time when he couldn't find bookings in vaudeville. As he himself said, "I might've starved that summer—or gone back to Bristol."

Later, in 1927, at another swanky dinner party, he met Reginald Hammerstein, who was a key player in Grant's segue from vaudeville to Broadway. Reginald introduced him to his powerful uncle, Arthur Hammerstein, who cast him in *Golden Dawn*, a musical comedy that opened the new Hammerstein Theatre in 1927. His part as an Australian prisoner of war was a small one, but it led to more work and eventually a lucrative stage contract. Archie Leach was on his way.

But it wasn't all smooth sailing. He might have been able to charm his way into high society, but fooling critics was another matter. His experience as a singer amounted to little more than belting out tunes with his balladeer dad at family gatherings and a few hastily arranged singing lessons to prepare him for his musical-comedy debut, which was hardly enough to light up the Great White Way.

"I realized," he recalled in Nancy Nelson's *Evenings with Cary Grant*, "that to get anywhere in my work, I had to go onto the legitimate stage. I began to do musical comedies—for less money than I had been earning. I was taking a chance because I had never done any serious singing. I sang only English music hall ballads, and those were mainly for my own amusement."

Reviewers quickly noticed his shortcomings and delighted in pointing them out. In a 1929 review of the play *A Wonderful Night*, which was based on Johann Strauss's *Die Fledermaus*, one critic noticed the jarring working-class element in the polished persona Archie was struggling to create: "Leach, who feels that acting in something by Johann Strauss calls for distinction, is somewhat at a loss as to how to achieve it. The result is a mixture of John Barrymore and Cockney."

But the bad reviews only motivated him to eradicate the flaws in his stage technique and personal style. Clearly, he had a lot to learn, and no one knew that better than he did.

The common wisdom about Cary Grant today is that his success was largely due to his godly good looks, but the real key to not only his stardom but to his personal happiness was a quality less tangible—namely, a lively curiosity, a love of learning that is at the heart of any keen intellect. Without it he could never have transformed himself into Cary Grant.

It's a trait that can be traced back to his earliest memories. "The most intriguing toy I ever got my hands on," he recalled, "was a pair of pinking scissors with which my mother made a crinkled edge on the shelving and table cloth. The symmetrical result fascinated me. I couldn't fathom how the scissors did it, and for practically one whole morning, while mother was out in the garden, I pinked edges on almost everything reachable, including my own nightshirt."

He was a willing student in all areas of his life, including his marriages. He said that he "remained deeply obliged" to his second wife, Barbara Hutton, long after they divorced, "for a welcome education in the beauties of the arts and other evidences of man's capability for gracious expression and graceful living."

From Barbara Harris Grant, his fifth wife, he learned probably the greatest lesson of all: how to be happy. He called her his "best piece of magic."

Professionally, directors, particularly George Cukor, contributed a great deal to the Cary Grant style. In 1936, while making *Sylvia Scarlett*, Cukor said that Grant was initially "rather wooden," but by the end of the shoot, he had "suddenly burst into bloom." Grant went on to make some of his most popular pictures with Cukor, including *The Philadelphia Story*, with Katharine Hepburn and Jimmy Stewart.

Grant is regarded as the first actor to thumb his nose at studio control freaks and take his chances as a freelancer. Although his decision to break ties in 1936 with the Paramount safety net was a risky and unprecedented move for an actor who hadn't yet reached the A-list, it was by no means an impulsive one. It wasn't based on greed or youthful arrogance or blind ambition. His independence at such an early time in his career was a well-informed risk, for he had aligned himself, at least psychologically, with the mavericks of the industry. He was never one to aim low. Charlie Chaplin, Douglas Fairbanks Sr., and Mary Pickford had formed United Artists, the first production company conceived by actors. They were his business as well as artistic inspirations. They, said Grant, "not only studied their craft thoroughly and made films of their own choosing—quite successfully, too, according to the public's reaction—but banded together to manage their own studio, distributing company and circuit of theaters as well."

UA would become the model on which Grant's own production companies, Granart and Granox, would produce some of his most successful films, including *Indiscreet*, *That Touch of Mink*, and *Operation Petticoat*.

Historically Mae West might not be remembered as much of a mentor, but she taught Grant, if only by example, about the finer points of deal making, Hollywood style, and the intricacies of comic timing.

She received not only creative control but a percentage of the profits as well as a sizeable salary for *She Done Him Wrong*, a highly unusual arrangement for a star, especially a female one.

Even though he was only twenty-eight years old at the time they worked together, an age when most actors are more entranced by Hollywood's bevy of beauties than balance sheets, Grant took note of West's contractual shrewdness. As soon as he acquired the proper leverage, he negotiated for not only a salary but a percentage of each film's gross. In some cases he did this so well he earned more money than the producers or directors associated with his films, including powerhouses like Alfred Hitchcock.

By the late 1940s, when he was a big star, Grant became one of Hollywood's most incisive deal makers, revealing almost visionary business acumen. His contracts stipulated that the negatives of his films revert to him seven years after their initial release; studio executives and bean counters never even put up a fight about this particular clause. Who would want to watch a picture after seven years, they reasoned? Well, millions of people, as it turned out. When television came on the scene in the early 1950s, Cary Grant movies were in great demand for slots on late-night TV. He reaped a steady windfall from the lucrative licensing fees generated by the rights of the films he controlled.

"I remember mentioning *Penny Serenade* in the late seventies," recalls Peter Bogdanovich, "and he said, 'Oh, yes, I just got a check on that one,' and I thought, Jesus, that was in 1941 and he'd already gotten a piece of the action."

Grant's love of learning continued long after he retired from making movies.

In a *GQ* profile published in 1986, the year he died, he was still picking up style tips from powerful men like Aristotle Onassis and Lew Wasserman. "Those characters," he said, "always wore dark-blue suits."

In the 1980s he traveled the country for "A Conversation with Cary Grant," a stage appearance that featured Grant's favorite film clips followed by a question-and-answer period, an experience he greatly enjoyed and one that was immensely successful even though he had not made a movie in more than a decade.

Film critic David Thomson spoke to him after one of these appearances in San Francisco. "Even then," recalls Thomson, "and he must've been in his late seventies, he didn't want to hear how great he was, what a legend he was, or how great his body of films was. He asked me over and over how I thought he could improve the show, how he might make it better, what could he change to make audiences happier. But he was absolutely great in it."

This was not Grant's purported perfectionism rearing its ugly head. It was something else entirely.

CG and Katharine Hepburn in
Philadelphia Story (1941).

THE SHIRT OFF HIS BACK

*"They're such beautiful shirts,"
she sobbed, her voice muffled in
the thick folds. "It makes me sad
because I've never seen such—
such beautiful shirts before."*

— F. SCOTT FITZGERALD, *THE GREAT GATSBY*

In this case the shirt off his back was forty years old. But it was a good shirt, top-notch, for it had been purchased from Hawes & Curtis, one of the most distinguished tailors and shirtmakers in London's West End.

The English poet Rupert Brooke wrote about "the good smell of old clothes." Men of style have always valued the comforting patina that age lends old clothes, the way they become happily molded to one's body, a kind of second skin.

Fred Astaire disliked the stiffness of his new hats and suits so much he tossed them against a wall to rid them of their annoying newness.

Old clothes have another appeal. They are tried-and-true, reliable. They hold no surprises, for they are known quantities that greatly reduce the possibility of a "wardrobe malfunction," a great reassurance for anyone about to attend an important event.

And this was a very important event. It was 1978, Princess Caroline of Monaco was getting married, and Cary Grant wanted to wear his favorite evening shirt to the wedding.

But there was only one problem: the neck band was shot. So he picked up the phone in his Beverly Hills home and called Hawes & Curtis in London.

"I remember getting a phone call one morning," says Stephen Lachter, who was then the company's manager and now has his own company at 16 Savile Row, "and the voice on the other end saying 'Good morning, this is Cary Grant. I am going to send you an evening shirt that I would like a new neckband put on. Is that okay?' I was already making Frank Sinatra two new stiff-fronted formal dress shirts, as the wedding was to be white tie, that is, full dress tails, and I said, 'Yes,' and we chatted for a few moments about his requirements and I duly awaited receipt of the shirt."

But Lachter wasn't sure what to expect. His company had not made shirts for Cary Grant in ten years, so he assumed that perhaps the shirt in question had been made by someone else and all Grant wanted was a frayed neck band replaced.

When the shirt finally arrived, Lachter was amazed. "The label in the shirt," he says, "was Hawes & Curtis and it had the old Prince of Wales coat of arms on it, which meant that the shirt was actually made before Edward VIII became king, probably around nineteen thirty-four or thirty-five. Yes, he really did send me a forty-year-old shirt to repair!"

The transaction proved to be such a success that Lachter made several more evening shirts for the retired movie star. "They were always the same," he says, "white pleated voile, and he liked soft collars."

Mostly, they spoke over the phone. "He was always very polite, friendly, and courteous. I only ever met him once. He was a naturally good dresser, and this, I believe, came instinctively. He was never 'flash,' always classic, and I think the thing that made him stand out against other men was like all great dressers—simplicity—he never tried too hard."

CARY GRANT

24th January, 1983.

Dear Stephen Lachter,

As you will see, enclosed is the cheque for two hundred and fifty-five dollars ($255.00). This represents the full payment for the three evening shirts I ordered for my husband.

While on the telephone last week, we did discuss the slight problems that we have with the weight and size of the collars, however, you seemed to think this could be remedied when next we are in London.

Thanking you again for your assistant and looking forward to meeting you later this year,

Sincerely,

Mrs. Cary Grant.

FOUR

FROM FLAWS TO FLAWLESSNESS

"Style is by no means an adornment as some people think, it is not even a question of technique, it is—like color for painters—a quality of vision, the revelation of the particular universe which each of us sees, and which is not seen by others."—MARCEL PROUST

An awareness of personal flaws was far more useful, even essential, in the development of Cary Grant than flattery ever was. In fact it was the springboard to his most appealing features. His trademark manner of dress, for instance, derived directly from a flaw that is not even recognized today, the reason he flunked his first screen test.

In 1929 Oscar Serlin, a New York–based talent scout for Paramount, saw Grant in the Broadway musical *Boom Boom*. Impressed by the handsome young actor's charisma, he invited him to take a screen test in the studio's headquarters, in Astoria, Queens.

But Archie had no chemistry with the camera. What was an asset on Broadway was a liability on film. On stage, at six feet two inches and 180 pounds, he was a tall, dark, and strikingly handsome pres-

CG making the most of his Anglo roots in 1930s Hollywood. Here he wears a buttoned-up jacket with a Ghillie collar, a sort of Deeside or Tweedside coat, the antecedent of the modern lounge suit. The silk neckerchief adds panache to what would otherwise be a staid look.

ence, diminished to just the right proportion by the big cavernous Broadway theaters. On-screen, however, particularly in close-ups, the camera revealed what theater audiences couldn't see: a broad neck that measured seventeen and a half inches. Years of acrobatics had made him strong and fit, but they had also overdeveloped the muscles in his neckline. As a result the studio turned him down flat, adding that they thought he was "bow-legged and pudgy," to boot.

"I don't think any non-actor," said Grant years later, "can ever know how horrifying it is to hear your voice, see yourself, see how you walk, see every minute gesture enlarged on screen."

While other actors might have thrown in the towel and scurried away with their proverbial tails between their legs, their egos crushed by what seemed like a career-killing professional pronouncement, Archie Leach, though disappointed, was hardly thwarted by the criticism.

"My goal had always been to enhance and celebrate the natural body shape, but the human form so rarely matched that ideal. The 'natural' look was almost always illusion, a subtle manipulation of fabric and fantasy. The art of fashion was the appearance of ease, of effortless elegance."

— OLEG CASSINI

Always able to take a hard objective look at himself, he saw that they were right. He *did* have a thick neck. This marks another turning point in his personal style, for he was forced to do more than merely emulate people like Noel Coward and other style eminences of the day; he would need to formulate a sartorial philosophy based on his own peculiar physique.

He did this with the invaluable assistance of the world's finest tailors: Hawes & Curtis, Stephens & Co., Kilgour, French & Stanbury (all of London); and Bernard Wearthill, E. Tautz, and Lord (of New York), hallowed ground for men of style who understood their special parlance: "50 qualities and thousands of designs with a Royal Warrant of the Duke of Edinburgh"; "Finest Lairdsmoor Heather Hopsacking"; "Fine Lisle vat-dyed socks."

"With bespoke," explains Carlo Brandelli, Kilgour's current creative director, who has designed wardrobes for Jude Law and Hugh Grant, "we appreciate that every single customer is different." He continues: "The proportional equations that we have to work on with each body shape are always essentially the same. However, depending on how you stand and how your body actually is, each suit is going to be completely unique, so where the proportions are will vary from person to person, depending on height and width and size and many, many formulas which we have to take into account.

"Also, in cutting a very elegant suit there is something nondefinable that a tailor must have and that's what gives the suit and the wearer its panache. It's not something we can say is this formula—x plus y equals this—it's just an inner feeling of creativity that produces the best-looking suit for that shape."

From then on Archie Leach wore custom-made shirts with a tall collar to conceal his thick neck, a sartorial adjustment whose success had already been demonstrated by the aforementioned daring dresser Jack Buchanan.

Buchanan's neck was also slightly out of proportion to his body. It wasn't muscular like Archie's, but it was rather long, so Buchanan wore tab collars to disguise it, and set off a fashion trend in the process.

As it was then, so it is today. Author Tom Wolfe, known for his spiffy white suits as well as his best-selling novels and groundbreaking gonzo journalism, has a swanlike neck and favors collars that flatter what might not otherwise appear to be an attractive attribute.

According to Flusser, "Long-necked men welcome the tab's higher positioning, while the round or square-shaped visage appreciates its longitudinal symmetry."

Wolfe was and still is a fashion nabob, afflicted with what he called in his essay "The Secret Vice" a pleasant addiction to custom tailoring. He still delights in the art of fine menswear and has his clothing custom made in New York. "This is my third tailor," he says ruefully. "They keep going out of business. It's a dying art."

Wolfe lunched with Grant at the Plaza Hotel in 1963 for a profile that ran in the *New York Herald Tribune*, a meeting of two dandies, one would think, but they didn't talk about clothes.

"I was too outclassed," Wolfe says, laughing.

He describes Grant's clothes as "all worsteds, broadcloths and silks, all rich and underplayed, like a viola ensemble."

GRANT'S CUSTOM-MADE shirts were only the beginning, though. The shoulders of his Savile Row suits were also modified. And not just because of his thick neck. He had the narrow sloping shoulders of a gymnast, which not only made his neck look larger than it actually was but, as he himself admitted, accentuated an anatomically large head. When he watched himself on-screen, he said that he was "appalled by its size."

One of the few times it is evident, even glaring, to the viewer is in *Notorious*. In his first scene with Ingrid Bergman, he is seated with his back to the camera, a dark silhouette amid a throng of drunken revelers at a party that is fast winding down. He remains quiet, as still as a statue, his neck and head displayed above the crest of the chair like an onyx sculpture on a pedestal.

A mysterious presence, he almost seems inanimate. Although Hitchcock purposely and shrewdly chose this angle to create an ominous mood, Grant's thick neck and large head can clearly be seen from this rare but revealing perspective.

There was yet another physical defect that he would have to address—many others, in fact. One of his shoulders sloped lower than the other. Cary Grant, often perceived as the ideal male, was as far from Adonis-like perfection as any mere mortal.

BELOW

Grant with Ingrid Bergman and Alfred Hitchcock. His muscular neck is revealed in this rare photo of Grant wearing an open-collared shirt.

OPPOSITE

On screen, his stocky neck can be seen in this rear view of him in Notorious *(1946).*

Savile Row's particular brand of sartorial magic was harnessed to balance his thick neck and narrow shoulders with the rest of his body. This was accomplished by broadening the shoulders of his suits with padding to make his head appear smaller. The scyes—the tailor's technical term for armholes—were also adjusted; they were cut higher to make his silhouette look slimmer, less "pudgy," to use the term of the testy talent scouts.

A shirt with a higher collar and a stylish tie concealed his flaws and added prestige to his person. The tuxedo, with its high wing collar and the camouflaging aspects of the ascot, produced similar results. Henceforth they became wardrobe staples, particularly the tuxedo, which he seems to wear in every other movie, the closest thing to a sidekick he would ever have.

By the time he made *North by Northwest* in 1959, Grant's impeccable style was second nature to him.

Recalls Eva Marie Saint, his costar in the classic Hitchcock thriller, "After a day of shooting, we were all having dinner in Chicago one night, and we decided to go out to a nightclub to see I think it was Judy Garland. So everybody had to get dressed up—well, everybody except Cary. Cary was always beautifully dressed.

"But he wasn't a clotheshorse. We were talking on the plane going from Mt. Rushmore to Los Angeles, and he explained to me how he always packed light. His tastes were really simple, elegant but simple. And he seemed just as comfortable in a suit and tie as someone else would be in a pair of sweats. I can't even imagine him owning a pair of sweats or a T-shirt."

But he did. Sort of. Even when he donned a more casual look—slacks, pullover, and loafers, for instance, as he does in *To Catch a Thief*—he never abandoned the basic sartorial principles that were engendered by his flaws. Although Edith Head was in charge of that picture's wardrobe, Grant himself handpicked his resort-casual attire for a film that would be shot in Cannes and other picturesque south-of-France locations.

"Cary Grant, not having a stylist or someone dictating how he should dress, had to find his own path," says Brandelli, "which happened to be extremely elegant. And he knew about the details, whereas today, some movie stars are very happy to follow a director's vision of what should be elegant or stylish, or a stylist's version or a journalist's version."

The famous striped polo shirt that Grant wears with gray pleated slacks and loafers in *To Catch a Thief* would be stylish enough for most leading men, but Grant added a foulard neckerchief, which he found by combing the local shops, a personal touch that accomplished two things: it flattered his thick neckline and at the same time added panache to a plain outfit.

According to one critic, the look was so admired it set off a fashion trend that got out of hand: "If," wrote Charles Frazier in *Esquire*, "Cary Grant of *To Catch a Thief* was culpable of anything, it was less his onetime activities as a 'cat bur-

glar' than the fact that his clothes in that movie aroused such demonstrative admiration among women that any number of men were inspired to try to copy the actor's wardrobe. For the most part, the results were disastrous."

Everybody wants to be Cary Grant. . . .

A SIMPLE ACCESSORY, such as a silk neckerchief, can, as Grant demonstrated, work wonders to distinguish an outfit. And it still can. Just ask Jude Law.

"After we took the basic silhouette of Jude, which was essentially a slim elegant suit," says Brandelli, "the first thing I introduced was something that was more popular in the thirties and forties: a very simple and elegant silk scarf. I just put a scarf around his neck, and it launched a thousand looks."

CG in the famous striped pullover and foulard neckerchief. "Hitch," said Grant, "trusted me implicitly to select my own wardrobe. If he wanted me to wear something very specific he would tell me, but generally I wore simple, tasteful clothes—the same kind of clothes I wear offscreen."

Brandelli continues, "I've worked with Jude for many years now. The brief when we first started working together was to do something quite timeless and elegant in the tradition of somebody like Cary Grant, whose style was immediately understood and acknowledged; he was someone we spoke about a lot. Cary Grant is incredibly relevant today. He's one of three or four names which immediately come to mind when you think of style from a cinematic era."

But Cary Grant was as much at home dressing down as he was dressing up. He even managed to instill a certain sartorial eloquence to a plain shirt, as much a result of the way he wore it as the fact that it was custom made.

Instead of wearing shirts with the collar splayed across his chest, he fastened them to the top or next-to-the-top button and turned up the back of the collar, yet another concession to his neckline. The upturned collar disguised what was probably no longer a thick neck—he had slimmed down by the late 1930s—but it was an attribute about which he was always self-conscious.

CG in The Bishop's Wife *(1947) wearing a patterned scarf that inspired Carlo Brandelli of Savile Row's Kilgour to create a similar look for Jude Law.*

A rare candid photo of Grant from 1955 (page 71, lower right) plainly shows his habit of wearing a turned-up collar. The interesting thing is that even wearing the most mundane attire, he never loses his Cary Grantness.

Such was the case on-screen as well. In *Houseboat*, which costarred Sophia Loren, there's a scene in which he's dressed in work clothes, preparing to tackle the chore of painting the dilapidated houseboat on which he, a single father, lives with his three children and their "maid," sexy Sophia. His blue shirt is buttoned to the neck, and the back of the collar is turned up (page 71, top).

In the climactic scenes of *To Catch a Thief*, when he's scaling shadowy rooftops in hot pursuit of the thief for whose crimes he is blamed, he is dressed in what many viewers mistakenly thought was a black turtleneck (page 70), but it is actually a dark shirt worn in his unique way: the up-turned collar covers his neck so completely it might as well *be* a turtleneck.

The basic tenets of this look were followed so consistently that they are even evident in his sleepwear. In *Houseboat* when he says good night to his children, he is wearing a pajama top that is buttoned to his Adam's apple; the back of the collar is again turned up, an odd but eye-catching look that is pure Cary Grant; even bedtime could not bedevil the man's sense of style.

"Cary Grant is incredibly relevant today. He's one of three or four names which immediately come to mind when you think of style from a cinematic era."

— CARLO BRANDELLI,
CREATIVE DIRECTOR,
KILGOUR, SAVILE ROW

And he's consistent. In a photo taken on the set of *Indiscreet* (page 71, bottom left), Grant exhibits the same sleepwear style.

At times the broad neck slips into view, either unintentionally or for the sake of a particular role. But it is rare. In *The Howards of Virginia* (1940), a costume drama in which Grant plays a Daniel Boone–type character, he wears a buckskin shirt open at the neck. There was just no way around it: after all, he couldn't very well sport a tweedy Savile Row suit and pin-dot tie for a story set in frontier America.

Some of his flaws were more difficult to disguise—some downright impossible. Like his smile. When he was a boy, he collided with another pupil while walking across a frozen playground. He slipped on the ice and hit the ground hard, snapping his front tooth in two. Afraid to burden his father with another bill, he went to a free dental clinic and had the other half removed.

The procedure left a large gap between his upper front teeth. Eventually the gap closed, leaving him with a set of irregularly placed teeth. It is ironic that a smile known for its movie-star flawlessness is, in fact, flawed (page 73).

But he did nothing to hide it. Unlike actresses such as Gloria Grahame, whose insecurities about her own smile led her to insert clumps of tissue in her

In all of these photos Grant reveals his habit of turning up his shirt collar to soften what he regarded as a flaw—a thick neck.

OPPOSITE
Negotiating a rooftop in To Catch a Thief *(1955) wearing a buttoned-up black shirt that some audiences mistakenly thought was a turtleneck.*

RIGHT
With Sophia Loren in Houseboat *(1958).*

BELOW
Filming Indiscreet *(1958).*

BELOW RIGHT
Holding the script for To Catch a Thief *(1955).*

mouth to plump up her lips, or today's stars, who resort to collagen injections for fuller lip lines, Cary Grant did the opposite. He put it on full display, smiling as if he possessed the best set of pearly whites in the business. In this photograph of Grant taken during the filming of *Charade*, in 1963 (opposite), when he was fifty-nine, the confidence and charm of his broad grin eclipse any flaws in his smile that might otherwise be evident.

Another attractive feature of Grant's that was devised as a result of an imperfection was his hair. It was parted on the wrong side of his head. Unlike his teeth, however, this was done purposely, at the behest of the tyrannical director Joseph von Sternberg during the filming of *Blonde Venus* in 1932. Von Sternberg, a visual master, noticed the actor's oddly proportioned head before they got past the first scene and immediately did something about it; he took a comb and parted Grant's hair on the right rather than the left side of his head, the opposite of the way Grant had worn it all his life. Von Sternberg's modification was a stroke of genius, for it improved the actor's looks in a way not even plastic surgery could have accomplished. This was not a temporary but a permanent change that gave Grant's face the illusion of symmetrical perfection with which it is associated today. As Audrey Hepburn says to him in *Charade*, as if voicing the audience's thoughts, "You know what's wrong with you? *Nothing*."

But of course those early talent scouts would disagree. Grant was, according to them, "bow-legged." Not an easy flaw to fix. But somehow he managed it. Like his irregular teeth, he chose not to hide this physical defect but to present it to the world as if it were something special.

The result was a light, athletic step infused with a kind of jaunty elegance. It was as amusing and as memorable to his fans as some of his best movies.

"When I got to know Cary, he was the youngest eighty-year-old I'd ever met," Ralph Lauren recalled in the documentary *A Class Apart*. "We were sitting at the track and he said, 'Ralph, would you like to take a walk' and he had the coolest, youngest walk, and so sprightly. It sort of inspired me to say remember what you saw because it was really great."

The pudginess that the talent scouts complained about was addressed more directly—with a combination of diet and exercise. In 1932 after he'd moved to Los Angeles, where Hollywood had changed its mind about him and signed him to a lucrative contract, he bought a spacious

CG in Charade *(1963). The seemingly perfect movie-star smile had been marred in a childhood accident, but he infused it with such warmth and charm no one noticed.*

beach house in Santa Monica, where his exercise routine consisted of an hour of weight lifting every morning followed by a refreshing dip in the ocean. He lifted weights twice a day, adding a session before going to bed. Lots of repetitions with light weights made him strong as well as lean.

Although some of his peers would be disappointed—such as Katharine Hepburn, who said she liked the way he looked when he had that chunky, slightly pudgy face—he became as lean and trim as a cyclist competing in the Tour de France, even in middle age.

HE ALSO BECAME health conscious long before it was fashionable, but never to the point where fitness wasn't fun. He had a running bet with Randolph Scott that the first one to exceed his designated body weight would have to pay the other one hundred dollars; later they upped the ante to one thousand dollars, with all proceeds going to charity.

But no money ever changed hands. Grant remained a trim 180 pounds, and Scott, whose dedication to staying in shape was as unbending as his friend's, never gained an ounce; so the result was a draw.

Compared to Grant's childhood experiences with exercise, these beachside workouts were a joy. Education in Edwardian England was extremely strict and included compulsory physical training every morning in a cold and damp court-yard followed by a rough-and-tumble game of football (or soccer, as Americans call it) in the chill or freezing rain of the afternoon.

This new SoCal lifestyle not only transformed his physique, but it also gave him a kind of boundless vitality and stamina that translated to the screen and was, as *Movieland* reporter Maureen Welsh observed when she visited Grant at RKO in 1944, equally evident when he wasn't filming. "He comes to work on his day off," she wrote. "All day long on the set, Cary's teeming with vitality, like a race horse champing at the bit. When the director calls him to go into a scene, he leaps onto the set, with his eyes shining, ready to act. In between shots he's everywhere, talking to everybody and deeply interested."

Grant also enjoyed horseback riding, especially later in life, when he would explore the trails along the San Jacinto Mountains near his Palm Springs home.

But probably the favored and most vigorous exercise of all was chasing women. Women, he often said, were one of his "favorite causes."

As can be seen in this early photo from the 1930s of Grant in front of his Santa Monica beach house (below), he's trim, congenial, and active. Early home movies of this period show girls in swimsuits scurrying in and out of the house he shared with dreamboat actor Randolph Scott. David Niven and Errol Flynn shared a house in the neighborhood, as did other notorious playboys who made up a kind of British Rat Pack. Their bachelor digs became weekend retreats for starlets and actresses who attended their lavish poolside parties, barbecues, and long afternoons of leisurely sunbathing by the sea.

Grant was linked to many beautiful women of the early 1930s and eventually married one of them, a stunning blonde by the name of Virginia Cherrill. A glamorous high-society type, she became Grant's first wife, in 1934. She was also an actress. Best known for her role as the blind girl in Charlie Chaplin's *City Lights*, she left Hollywood shortly after the couple divorced, following fewer than two years of marriage, and devoted the rest of her life to humanitarian causes. They remained close friends and confidants. Grant greatly admired her selflessness and gave her a spot on his list of twelve ideal female dinner companions decades after their parting.

Grant's diet was simple—and enviably effective. He ate whatever he wanted but always in moderation. When Tom Wolfe lunched with him in the Plaza Hotel's Edwardian Room, he noted that Grant's meal consisted of "a single bowl of Vichyssoise."

According to his friend Roderick Mann, Grant preferred simple fare, especially the kind of pub food he ate as a boy growing up in England: bangers and mash, shepherd's pie, toast and tea,

An early snapshot of a young GG in front of his Santa Monica beach house.

scones and marmalade. But he was not at all averse to gourmet dishes. Angie Dickinson once remarked that he could eat caviar by the bucketful.

Even well into his seventies, he remained trim, avoiding the bloated fate of many of his fellow Hollywood retirees. He said that whenever he gained a few pounds, he simply scaled down the size of his meals until he returned to a satisfactory weight.

But he always told reporters that he disliked exercise and did very little of it, except for occasional outings on horseback. The claim is true, but it applies only to his later years. In *To Catch a Thief*, he rises out of the ocean in front of the Carlton Hotel and walks toward the beach, tugging on his swim trunks, his body glistening in the sun, his back as muscular and rippled as Richard Gere's in his *American Gigolo* prime. Grant was fifty then, an age when not even the best genes in the world can produce such a well-chiseled physique without at least some effort.

To Grant, revealing such personal details about himself, even something as trivial as what he ate for breakfast, was unseemly, a breach of one's privacy and a kind of moral transgression. When Sophia Loren wrote about their affair in her autobiography, he reputedly thought this the ultimate betrayal, and their friendship suffered because of it. He rarely if ever gossiped about other people, certainly not to the press, and lived by the old adage that if you don't have anything good to say about someone, then you shouldn't say anything at all.

Grant had also been an early exponent not only of moderation in diet but of a healthy all-around lifestyle. At one time a two-pack-a-day smoker, he gave up what he called the "filthy habit" in the 1940s, a period when everybody smoked, even old ladies and grandmothers, and he frequently lectured friends about its dangers.

"Do you know you're killing yourself?" he would say to just about anybody who went near a cigarette, even the regal Jackie Onassis, who visited him at his Beverly Hills home. When she asked for a light, he refused to find her one.

But his hard-nosed self-discipline paid off. In 1957 *Newsweek* called him a "rakish Hollywood star who simply won't grow old." His favorite leading lady, Grace Kelly, agreed. "Everyone grows older," she said, "except Cary Grant."

Myrna Loy, Grant's costar in *The Bachelor and the Bobby-Soxer* and *Mr. Blandings Builds His Dream House*, met him at a 1981 MGM luncheon held in her honor and was awed by his youthful vigor. He was seventy-seven years old.

"Cary looked marvelous that day," she wrote in her autobiography. "It was the first time we had met since he had taken another young wife. 'Congratulations, you old fool,' I chided, grabbing a bicep. Solid as a rock, I observed."

HE HAD COME a long way since his first screen test. He had evolved from a supposedly flawed stage actor unsuitable for film to a style icon as well as a great actor, and a defiantly ageless one at that.

His ascent had been a rapid one, too. In 1932 he had so firmly grasped what Tom Wolfe called "the marginal differences" in men's tailoring, the subtle details that distinguish bespoke from ready-made clothes, that he confidently went into the business. He invested in a men's apparel shop called Neale, at 3161 Wilshire Boulevard. Although the store eventually went bust, Grant's interest in clothes remained undiminished. Throughout his life he would keep abreast of fashion trends, jotting notes to Yves Piaget, Vidal and Beverly Sassoon, Pierre Cardin, and other designers complimenting them on their work. He wrote to fashion designer Amir saying that he admired his "passion for fashion." He sang Ralph Lauren's praises before everybody else jumped on the bandwagon, and he sent him numerous articles mentioning Polo. "Dear Cary," writes Lauren in one letter, dated March 1979, "I subscribe to a monthly clipping service, but I think I shall discharge them. You do a far better job than they do, in fact I would say a superb one."

And he sent letters to his old friend Oleg Cassini with remarks that revealed that he still had a keen and interested mind about the world of fashion.

By the 1950s Grant had become so sure of himself that he started second-guessing the Savile Row experts with whom he had collaborated for many years.

Jack Taylor, who at eighty-six still goes to work every morning at his custom men's tailoring store located next to Spago in Beverly Hills, first met Grant in the early 1950s.

"I was working as a tailor in New York at the time, and he wanted me to take in the pants of a suit he had just had made in London," recalls Taylor, who counts Frank Sinatra and Elvis Presley among a long list of celebrity clientele. "The style then for pants was baggy, but he wanted them slimmer. He was very tall, and he decided that the slim cut was a better look for him, and he was right. But this was before slimmer pants were popular. He knew what looked good on him, regardless of trends or the style of the day and went with it. He knew a lot about the technical details of clothing too. He had been going to English tailors for years by then."

This was not a practice without precedent. The Duke of Windsor also had his suit jackets made by a tailor in Savile Row and his trousers by a tailor in New York. In an era when men of true style reigned, going to such lengths to achieve the desired fit of one's clothing was not considered fussy or eccentric; it was just a matter of course. And it was by no means a sacrosanct subject. In fact it was occasionally a cause for some good-natured kidding. Wallis Simpson, the Duchess of Windsor, the duke's wife, humorously referred to her husband's trouser arrangement as "pants across the ocean."

Grant even handed out sartorial advice to his own doctor. In the early sixties, along with dozens of other Hollywood stars, Grant underwent a series of therapeutic LSD sessions supervised by Dr. Mortimer Hartman. He admired Hartman's intellect but somewhat jokingly suggested that he should "dress better."

Grant remembered Hartman in his will; perhaps the money was meant as a further incentive for the good doctor to improve his wardrobe.

As Tom Wolfe explained in his essay "The Secret Vice," "Once you know about it, you start seeing it. All the time! There are just two classes of men in the world, men with suits whose buttons are just sewn onto the sleeve, just some kind of cheapie decoration, or—yes!—men who can unbutton the sleeve at the wrists because they have real buttonholes and the sleeve really buttons up."

Once such knowledge is acquired, the difference between ready-made and bespoke clothes can be glaring. "They make armholes about the size of the Holland Tunnel," Wolfe wrote. "Anybody can get in these coats . . . this coat is loose and sloppy. . . . That's why custom-made suits have high armholes; because they fit them to a man's own particular shoulder and arm. And then all these other little details . . . practically all of these details follow the lead of English tailoring. . . . The shoulders are padded to give the coat shape; 'natural shoulders' are for turkeys and wet smacks."

Grant had reached a point in his life where he had mastered these finer points of style, and those who had not were aesthetically offensive to him, sort of sartorial cripples who elicited his sympathies and assistance, whether solicited or not. But he offered his help charitably. He liked beautiful things in all facets of his life and enjoyed sharing his pleasure in clothes with others.

He was by no means a sartorial snob, though. Peter Bogdanovich recalls in *Who the Hell's In It* that Grant "took one look at my jacket and said, 'Brooks Brothers?' I said yes, surprised. 'Right off the rack, isn't it?' I nodded. 'Yeah, I do the same thing. Fits perfectly.'"

He knew that the best clothing is not necessarily the most expensive. Some fashion purists were appalled at his ventures to Asia for better deals on his custom-made suits.

"Something of a maverick as to tailors," griped *Esquire*, "he now goes to Quintino in Beverly Hills, CA, and, whenever possible, certain of the preposterously low-priced geniuses in Hong Kong."

ONCE GRANT'S personal style was formulated, once it was no longer a goal in itself, it would become an expression of the inner man, a creative outlet that asserted his independence and artistry above and beyond the limits of his chosen profession. He no longer would be a Noel Coward wannabe, no longer a style emulator but a style innovator, a fashion icon whose stature, unlike his fashionable peers, would grow, not diminish, with age.

And, yes, nylon panties played a part in it.

A Suitable Profession... Or, The Man in the Worsted Wool Suit

"To dress well was a ritual and a passion; to dress well was like being in love."
—Oleg Cassini

This is a very revealing photo. It shows Cary Grant at a picnic, a rained-out picnic that has been moved indoors. He is flanked by his then-wife, Betsy, and a close friend, Fleur Cowles Meyer. It's his one day off from a grueling week of location shooting in Spain for *The Pride and the Passion.* Though this is a candid shot, not a posed publicity still, he's impeccably dressed—clean shaven in a charcoal gray suit, white shirt and cuff links, perfectly draped ascot, and gray socks, socks that somehow defy gravity and rise up seemingly to his torso, covering every inch of ankle and calf; not a bit of flesh is showing, no easy trick while sitting on the floor in an awkward crouch that would have upset the attire of even the most accomplished yogi.

Most movie stars today can't even cross their legs on a comfortable couch next to Jay Leno without showing that hairy divider between socks and pants—what former *Esquire* cofounder Arnold Gingrich thought of as "the line between the men and the boys in the art of wearing clothes: the avoidance of the exposure

of a length of bare calf between sock-top and trouser-bottom when seated."

But Cary Grant, despite the run through the rain, the hard seat on the hotel floor, and an unwieldy-looking sandwich, could not look more like Cary Grant—and on a day when he didn't have to. This was a candid snap, a vacation photo, taken by a friend. There was no time for primping or the intervention of a personal hair stylist, makeup artist, and personal lighting technician.

Yet there he is, resplendent, the man in the worsted wool suit, smiling congenially as if that hardwood floor was as cushy as a beanbag, his suit as comfortable and as comforting as a pair of well-worn jeans and a favorite old sweater.

This photograph illustrates perhaps better than any movie scene or posed publicity still his relationship with clothes. They were a natural extension of himself, sort of like B. B. King and his guitar, Yo-Yo Ma and his cello, Emeril and his pepper mill. They completed him, gave him the confidence to present himself to the world without ambivalence. Clothes were a kind of antidote to his shyness and self-doubts.

To be sure they are very nice clothes, custom-made clothes, straight from Savile Row, pricey and expertly pressed, but on CG they don't shout money or flash. They whisper quality and good taste. He made the clothes speak for him in a language of his own devising.

It might be said that he lived in an era when men tended to dress well, even when they were on a picnic. Although this was a time when men were seldom seen in public without a coat and tie, there were plenty of slobs among the stylish and those who dressed down when they were away from prying eyes, especially on their day off from work or when kicking back on vacation.

And then there were those who were well turned out but hated it—the Tom Raths of the world, the put-upon hero of Sloan Wilson's 1955 novel *The Man in the Gray Flannel Suit*, whose clothes symbolize stultifying male conformity, whose suit was a prison, not a pleasure; a garment to escape, not to celebrate.

It is significant to note that the movie version of *The Man in the Gray Flannel Suit*, starring Gregory Peck, was released the very year this photo was taken (1956). The book was published a year before, and both were huge popular successes.

So how did Cary Grant transcend the tenor of the times and make a formal look seem casual, relaxed, and most of all *fun*? How did he avoid seeming snobby or stuffy, foppish or fussy? After all, he's at a picnic, not a Hollywood premiere, in a suit no less, not the typical casual wear for such a function even back then.

One clue to his style is the jaunty air that undercuts any potential aristocratic pretense. Another is that when it comes to clothes, he's the boss—or as the fashion police like to say, "He wears the clothes; the clothes don't wear him."

Another trademark touch is the way he tempers the up-market Anglo with a healthy infusion of sporty Americanism: the broad open grin, the disarming friendliness, the one-of-the-guys amiability.

But the really important thing, the key to it all, is that the clothes make him happy. That was part of his art, the ability to wear clothes, all clothes—bespoke clothes from Savile Row's Kilgour, French, and Stanbury or an off-the-rack Brooks Brothers blazer—with appreciative joy.

True, a lot of time and care went into matching the ascot with the pocket square, searching for the right light-colored gray socks to contrast with the dark shoes and dark pants so that the transition from foot to ankle to leg was smooth and graceful. And yes, the clothes were impeccably cut, stylish, and *new* (or at least they appeared that way), but the *je ne sais quoi*, that special something that set him apart from other stylish men of the era—and there were quite a few, notably Fred Astaire, Tyrone Power, and Clark Gable—as well as the legions of Tom Raths, was the pleasure he derived from dressing well. Cary Grant loved clothes, and as we see in these rare photos, they returned the sentiment.

FIVE

ICON ASCENDING

"It was Cary Grant's innate sense of how to be a man that transcended everything else beyond his looks and even what he wore. Obviously the cut of his clothing is incredibly important, and we can talk all day about how elegant we could make somebody look, but if you don't understand intrinsically how to behave as a gentleman then the finest suits in the world would do very little for you."

—CARLO BRANDELLI, CREATIVE DIRECTOR, KILGOUR, SAVILE ROW

CARY GRANT did not wear boxers. Cary Grant did not wear briefs. Cary Grant wore women's nylon panties.

Long before Calvin Klein and the other design geniuses on Fashion Avenue set off a menswear revolution by creating the skimpy men's brief, a formfitting alternative to baggy boxers, and advertising it with the help of half-naked male models pictured on Times Square billboards, Cary Grant had already conceived of a nontraditional approach to bulky male undergarments.

His motivations were not kinky but purely practical. "I like them because they're cooler than men's underwear and they're so much easier to wash," he explained.

The Pride and the Passion *(1957), though not loved by critics, was a box-office hit and secured Grant's position on the list of Hollywood's top ten male stars. Once again the military uniform enhances his manly appeal.*

And easier to pack, too, a valued trait for a man who traveled light. Wash them by hand at night, wear them again the next day, and eliminate the need for suitcase-clogging multiple pairs.

Moreover, they were much more comfortable and flattering to a man's anatomy than boxers. According to Maureen Donaldson, who dated Grant in the 1970s, "they looked just like men's swimming trunks; they were hardly lacy or frilly. He was clearly wearing them for utilitarian reasons."

Boxer shorts, as any man who has worn them knows, tend to bunch up in the crotch and form unsightly bulges. Nylon panties have a form-flattering advantage, as any woman who has worn them knows; they also lift and give shape to the buttocks.

But men reap a special advantage from them: they create a compact orderliness to their frontal anatomy. In *The Pride and the Passion*, which costarred Frank Sinatra, Grant's choice of formfitting undergarments served him well, for his manhood is impressively adumbrated underneath the pants of his white naval uniform, a sign of virility that suits the role he is playing.

Cary Grant and Frank Sinatra were lifelong friends in real life, but in the 1957 adventure flick The Pride and the Passion, *they were rivals.*

THIS SARTORIAL TRICK was no secret: he shared it with his fellow actors, even encouraged it. When Peter Bogdanovich directed *What's Up, Doc?* (1972), he asked Grant to meet with Ryan O'Neal, his male star, to give him some pointers. Grant happily obliged, but when Ryan returned after a tête-à-tête with the legendary actor, he said that the only advice Grant had given him was to wear silk underpants.

Grant had reached a point in his life where he could create stylistic innovations peculiar to his own needs without feeling ashamed about their inspirational origins, even when they came from a less-than-manly source, like ladies' lingerie.

In fact he was so confident about his masculinity that he quite proudly announced his quirky preference during an interview for a 1960 best-dressed list compiled by *Esquire*. The magazine reported quite matter-of-factly that Grant "finds the most comfortable (and functional) of all underwear to be women's nylon panties" but oddly took him to task for favoring "such abominations as large tie knots."

> *. . . Grant "finds the most comfortable (and functional) of all underwear to be women's nylon panties."*
>
> — ESQUIRE MAGAZINE

Elvis used Clairol to dye his hair jet black. Tony Curtis used eyeliner to accent his eyes. And Cary Grant wore glute-enhancing panties.

It's ironic that the road to manly reinvention is littered with beauty products appropriated from the aisles reserved for female consumers, that masculinity is empowered by feminine underpinnings, and its ideal is created at least in part by elements typically associated with feminine allure.

THIS KEEN ATTENTION to personal appearance begs the question of whether Cary Grant was a metrosexual, the first fashion-forward man to use feminine techniques to enhance his own virile appeal.

After all, his fanatical devotion to suntanning is a practice held in high esteem by today's high-maintenance male.

But Cary Grant tanned for professional reasons. Vanity didn't much enter into it. He disliked pancake makeup not only because it looked fake on film but because it stained his clothing. He especially didn't like his leading ladies caked in Max Factor because their body makeup would sometimes soil his custom-made suits, which, by contract, reverted to him after the film wrapped.

A deep tan allowed him to sidestep this messy aspect of filmmaking. However, he was always thoughtful of others. Not wanting to put the makeup staff out of work, he'd let them do their thing and then discreetly wipe off the greasepaint.

Ingrid Bergman was an actor after his own heart. "I was very fond of Ingrid," he once said. "She was an amazing woman. . . . She used no makeup, not even lip rouge. Why don't more actresses imitate her instead of going the other way? You can tell how secure a woman is by the amount of makeup she wears."

The tan afforded him another advantage; it created an appealing contrast to his fair-skinned leading ladies. Grant chose his own wardrobe with the same aesthetic in mind, especially in the days of black-and-white movies, when the dark textures dramatically enhanced the lighter ones.

A tan also gave him a feeling of confidence and good health that he associated with Douglas Fairbanks Sr. and other manly models of silver-screen style and virility.

Most of all, his fondness for the sun harkened back to his early childhood, long before his fateful meeting with Fairbanks: "I first saw the light of day—or rather the dark of night—around 1:00 AM on a cold January morning in a suburban stone house which, lacking modern heating conveniences, kept only one step ahead of freezing by means of small coal fires in small bedroom fireplaces; and ever since, I've persistently arranged to spend every possible moment where the sun shines warmest."

In places where the sun didn't shine warmest, he still managed to make the most of whatever sunlight was available. In gray New York City, for instance, where as a spokesperson for Faberge Cosmetics he received the perk of a suite at the Warwick Hotel, he chose a room with a wraparound balcony that facilitated his ritual of daily sunbathing.

This amenity, however, did not always yield the desired results. One bright afternoon, stretched out on a lounge chair happily soaking up the sun's rays, he was disturbed by a tapping sound that quickly increased to what he called "a chorus of crickets." The women who worked in the skyscrapers that overlooked the hotel had discovered him and were trying to get his attention by telegraphically tapping the glass that enclosed their offices. There were dozens of them, each unaware of the other, an absurdity that amused the sunning septuagenarian.

Although he said it was "flattering but frustrating," that was the end of his sunbathing, at least on weekdays.

And nothing but natural sunlight would do. He disliked the brush-on tanning gels popular in his day. He thought their results "looked artificial."

He also liked to shop, a favorite metrosexual pastime. But according to Oleg Cassini, shopping back in Grant's day was a kind of art form: "We shopped. We spent whole afternoons shopping, but not as it is done today. It was an entirely different sort of experience—Socratic, almost religious, an extended negotiation over the most basic details: fabric, cut, stitching. We were the architects of our appearance; we supervised each new suit the way an architect guides the construction of a building."

Grant's childhood diaries testify to an early interest in this activity. In 1918, at the age of fourteen, he recorded these entries in his Boy Scout's journal: "14 Monday. After school I went and bought a new belt. And a new tie. . . . 19 Saturday. Had a new suit. A new pair of shoes. And a new cap. Seen show. In evening went to the Empire. 20 Sunday, second after Epiphany. Wore new suit. Went out to tea."

Later in life, as a wealthy movie star and successful businessman, he would shop in the most exclusive showrooms in the world. Unlike today, when designer stores are seemingly in every corner of the country, from Staten Island to Palm Desert, Grant had to travel the world to piece together a wardrobe that met his high standards.

The Burlington Arcade in London was a favorite haunt. He was such a frequent visitor to Aquascutum, where he bought suits, overcoats, and accessories, that he was often greeted by the chairman of the company, Sir Charles Abrahams.

Cashmere sweaters were carefully selected from N. Peal, and New Mown Hay, a favorite toilet water, was purchased at Floris. Green Irish Tweed by Creed was another favorite cologne.

Then it was off to Savile Row, a part of London with which he was intimately familiar, thanks to the Duke of Windsor, who had pointed the way when Grant was starting out in the 1920s—a period, according to Flusser, when "the American male was the beneficiary of some very favorable sartorial circumstances. The period began by catapulting the most important single force in modern men's fashion onto the world stage."

WALK, DON'T RUN. *A shopping spree with Cary Grant might entail visits to his favorite stores in London's Burlington Arcade (right) and then on to his Savile Row tailors and shirtmakers (page 90).*

That man was David, the Prince of Wales, aka the Duke of Windsor, who is probably best known for his scandalous decision in 1936 to abdicate the throne of England to marry the woman he loved, the American divorcée Mrs. Wallis Simpson. But when Grant first encountered him, he was a menswear trendsetter and considered by some experts to be a sartorial genius.

"In terms of dress the Duke of Windsor took no shortcuts, although his trick was to make it seem so," Cassini recalled in his autobiography, *In My Own Fashion*. "His intention was to give the appearance of nonchalance. Indeed, this—I have always believed—was the essence, the definition of style: feeling that no effort at all had been expended in selecting the paisley tie and checked jacket that just happened to go together perfectly. The Duke of Windsor cared tremendously about appearances, of course, but affected an attitude of *je ne sais quoi*, of casual abandon, of effortless grace."

In 1924, when Grant was making his transition from vaudeville comic to suave Broadway leading man, the towheaded heir to the throne of England made the rounds of Palm Beach parties, New York nightclubs, and lunches with President Calvin Coolidge. His movements were obsessively chronicled by magazines like *Men's Wear*, which reported that "the average young man in America is more interested in the clothes of the Prince of Wales than in any other individual on earth."

Archie Leach was one of those young men. Fairbanks's example had showed him the great appeal of the fit physique, the suntan, and a poised presence, but it was the Duke of Windsor who showed him that a serious understanding of clothes can add authority and dignity to the wearer.

> "Savile Row is the apotheosis of taste and elegance, all of which were virtues of Cary Grant," says Andrew Ramroop of Savile Row's Maurice Sedwell Ltd.
>
> — ESQUIRE MAGAZINE

"Savile Row is the apotheosis of taste and elegance, all of which were virtues of Cary Grant," says Andrew Ramroop of Savile Row's Maurice Sedwell Ltd. "He leapt beyond the boundaries of fashion by creating his very own style and derived great value out of his clothes by conscientiously selecting fabrics that were classics and outstanding in design and cut. His style has longevity because he drew attention not for his fashionable dressing but for his style and elegance."

The Prince of Wales also showed the eager student of style the way to Piccadilly; Jermyn Street, the traditional destination for fine men's shirts; Mayfair, where Grant shopped at such renowned establishments as Stephens & Co., whose clients included Grant's close friends Lord Mountbatten and Frank Sinatra; and Turnbull & Asser, a favorite stop for Prince Charles, also a friend.

Fred Astaire, whose name appeared regularly on the best-dressed lists of the time, had his suits made at Hawes & Curtis as well as Kilgour, tailors with whom Grant would have fruitful associations.

"I believe Cary Grant," says Noll Uloth, managing director of Cordings Ltd., one of London's most distinguished gentleman outfitters and shirtmakers, "did purchase raincoats from Cordings on a recommendation from the then Prince of Wales (the Duke of Windsor)."

Cordings, which was established in 1839, is famous for its mac and Covert coats and still draws some of the best-dressed men in the world through its doors, many of them celebrities. In fact legendary musician and man of style Eric Clapton is a part owner of the company.

Grant made his shopping sprees to England more enjoyable by combining them with visits to his favorite restaurants, such as the Guinea in Bruton Place and Claridges. He also had tea with old friends like Noel Coward and made side trips to Bristol to visit his mother and cousins.

In Rome he had suits made by Schiaparelli; when in New York he went to Dunhill's. In Los Angeles his favorite department store was Robinsons in Beverly Hills. Regardless of how much his wealth grew, he adhered to a simple but highly disciplined philosophy of shopping that his mother had passed on to him as a boy when they roamed the local shops together. He rarely bought anything after the first viewing, no matter how tempting the merchandise. This served two purposes: it avoided impulsive expenditures and tested the true appeal of the targeted item.

Sometimes his shopping was done over the phone. According to attorney William McIntosh and William Weaver, Grant's assistant in the 1970s (the authors of *The Private Cary Grant*), "[his] shirts were made for him by a special tailor in Spain or by a man called Tani in Tokyo with whom Grant had entered into negotiations many years before. Grant would order, over the phone, a selection of striped and colored shirts. When they arrived, he tried each on, with loving concentration. If they were anything short of perfect, they went back to Japan for alteration, and Grant would phone Tani his fresh specifications: 'extend the collar tip by ⅛ inch' would be the kind of request that would necessitate a 10,000-mile return journey."

CG and Joan Fontaine in Hitchcock's Suspicion *(1941).
"I'm sticking with the classics, and if somebody doesn't
like it, I can deal. If you look at Cary Grant's suits from
the thirties, forties, and fifties, they still look good today.
That's style, not fashion."*
—GLENN O'BRIEN, THE STYLE GUY

To some this practice might appear excessively fussy, almost obsessive-compulsive. But all great artists realize that even the smallest details are keenly important to the larger creation. In fact they *are* the larger creation.

"To be really great in little things," wrote Harriet Beecher Stowe, "to be truly noble and heroic in the insipid details of everyday life, is a virtue so rare as to be worthy of canonization."

GRANT ESPECIALLY LIKED to shop with his leading ladies. In 1962 he visited the New York showroom of Norman Norell with Doris Day to help her choose a suit and an evening gown that she wore in *That Touch of Mink*.

But the intrusion of fans and autograph seekers often interfered with these outings the way it did with his sunbathing. Tom Wolfe recalled Grant wistfully staring into the window of Bonwit Teller in New York City, unable to enter and browse like an ordinary person because of the chaos his presence would create if he dared to walk down the menswear aisles.

Bloomingdales, however, figured a way around this. They allowed him to shop when the store was shut to the general public, a privilege reserved for only a special few, and one he greatly enjoyed.

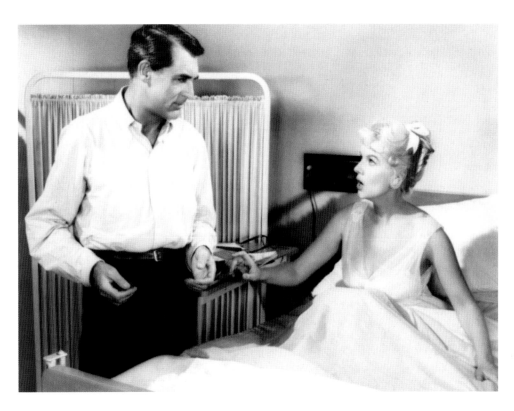

At home, though, there was nothing to prevent him from enjoying the pleasures of the fine wardrobe he had amassed over the years.

According to McIntosh and Weaver, "When clothes returned from the cleaners, Grant liked them to be left folded on his bed so that he could put them away exactly as he liked them, in his cupboards, hanging on wishbone hangers. Only he knew how to control these immense cupboards, since they were operated by electronic switches hidden under the carpet. Open, they were a vision of sartorial splendour, with row upon row of dark suits, dating back over several decades, and below them lines of highly polished custom-made shoes, one almost identical to the next."

This might seem like metrosexual heaven, but compared with the dandies of his day, Grant's habits were really quite tame. A preference for nylon stretch panties seems like a simple concession to the improvement of men's underwear when likened to the practice of London dandy Freddie Cripps's refusal to have his underwear made anywhere except in Vienna, to which he frequently traveled for fittings.

Socialite Maurice Bosdari was equally obsessed with appearances. Oleg Cassini met him during the 1950s and considered him one of the best-dressed

THE MAN IN THE BROOKS BROTHERS SHIRT. *Not all of Grant's stylish wardrobe was custom made. "I recognized the shirt he puts on in the hospital scene in* North by Northwest *as being from Brooks Brothers," says Peter Bogdanovich.*

Brooks Brothers' ready-made shirts, especially its white button-down Pima broadcloth, were in a class by themselves in the 1960s.

ICON
ASCENDING

men he'd ever known. Bosdari went to extraordinary lengths to obtain the right fit of his clothing. He insisted on his lapels being "tortured."

According to Cassini, "He would manipulate them, crush them with his hands until they rolled just right. He said, 'Clothing must never seem new: it must look old, but not too old.' He was the type of man who would take a new pair of riding pants and jump into a tub of water with them so that they would take his shape. He would then emerge—relieved!—and say, 'Ah, now they're right. The natural crease.' He was tall, very distinguished, and quite meticulous, a former Italian cavalry officer . . . he had one topic of conversation: appearances. He thought of nothing else."

Grant might have got a little testy when another actor smudged his suit with pancake makeup, but he hardly went to the extremes of Maurice Bosdari or the celebrated English illustrator Max Beerbohm, who thought that any true man of style should never have "the incomparable set of his trousers spoilt by the perching of any dear little child upon his knee."

Or Beau Brummel—the dandy of all dandies—who took three hours to dress and refused to remove his hat to a lady lest he not be able to return it to his head at the same felicitous angle.

In fact, he [Grant] was quite proud of the patina of age and, once again, turned what might seem like a disadvantage into an advantage by simply adjusting his wardrobe choices.

Grant paid meticulous attention to his personal appearance, but he never went as far as someone like, say, Noel Coward, who in 1926 reportedly underwent the first face-lift. Grant avoided such extremes. He wouldn't even dye his hair. In fact he was quite proud of the patina of age and, once again, turned what might seem like a disadvantage into an advantage by simply adjusting his wardrobe choices. In the 1940s he wore dark suits to match his jet black hair, but in *North by Northwest* (1959) he switched to a mid-gray suit that attractively matched his graying temples. He took such matters seriously, but never too seriously. "And if your hair falls out a bit," he quipped, "nobody will notice."

ACCORDING TO *GQ* columnist Glenn O'Brien, "English aristocrats gave their suits to their valets to wear until the suits lost their crispness." Grant broke in his own suits and relished the practice.

Although Grant's love of clothes is well documented, it is easily trumped by record-company executive Ahmet Ertegun, the son of a Turkish ambassador to the United States, who came into the possession of an E. Tautz of London alpaca-lined suit once owned by A. J. Biddle, a philanthropist and socialite who was considered at one time to be the best-dressed man in America. Ertegun kept the venerable garment under lock and key. He wore it on special occasions and unveiled it to only a few worthy admirers who were capable of appreciating its hand stitching and fine tailoring.

Grant's attitude toward his collection of suits was far less precious. Rather than horde them, he often gave them away to his friends, or tried to. According to producer William Frye, who worked with Grant in the 1950s on the *Lux Radio Theatre* versions of *Mr. Blandings Builds His Dream House*, "One day he asked me to go with him to Lyons Moving & Storage on Santa Monica Boulevard. He said he wanted to get a few things out of storage. I was stunned to find that he had a room-size vault, and when an attendant opened the doors, I found myself looking at all the clothes Cary didn't have space for in his house. There must have been at least 250 suits, 50 to 75 overcoats, and dozens and dozens of jackets, shoes, and hats. He picked out a couple of the things he'd come for and then said, 'Do you see anything you want? Just take it.' Unfortunately, Cary Grant's jackets didn't fit me, or his suits, or his overcoats. I walked out as I had walked in, in my own seersucker jacket, gray flannels, and saddle shoes."

Grant's interest in clothes was passionate but hardly obsessive. The same cannot be said for the Duke of Windsor, who in his 1960 book, *A Family Album*, devotes more than half of its pages (84 out of 144) to clothes and tailors.

The row upon row of Grant's meticulously polished custom-made shoes in his electronically controlled closets might corroborate a statement he made to *GQ* in 1986: "I always fancied shoes," but it was hardly a passion that could rival Arnold Schwarzenegger's, who admitted to *Vanity Fair* that he was "a major shoe queen."

But Beau Brummel bests them both. The Beau, as he was known in nineteenth-century London, is rumored to have mixed champagne in his boot polish to give his footwear its special spellbinding luster. He was so fussy about the fit of his gloves that he had the fingers constructed by one tailor, the thumbs by another.

Although Grant enjoyed productive relationships with tailors who helped him develop an iconic style, Brummel's friend, the then Prince of Wales, seemed to have preferred them to his own family. He said he "would rather be amiable and familiar with his tailor than agreeable and friendly with the most illustrious members of the aristocracy."

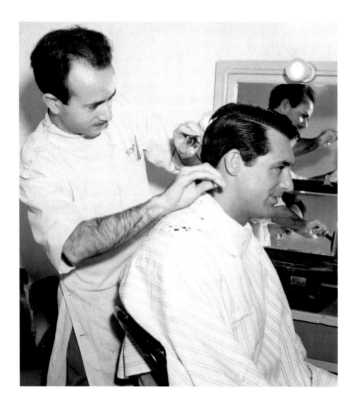

In the pre-metrosexual era, men like Grant went to a barber, not a salon, to get their hair cut.

Brummel changed his clothes three times a day and employed three different hair dressers simultaneously: one to temper the temples, another to care for the crown, and yet a third to fuss over the front.

Although Grant occasionally had his hair cut by the Plaza Hotel's legendary barber Vincent Battaglia, he more commonly patronized a neighborhood barber in Santa Monica, who cut his hair for six dollars.

BEAU BRUMMEL might seem like the most demanding of dandies by today's standards, but his reputation as a fashion icon is built on the radical simplicity he brought to men's dress. Prior to the Beau's entrance into high society, the *London Times* devoted as much space to the coverage of men's fashion as it did women's. Prince von Kaunitz, a favorite subject, typified the ostentation of the fashionable male; he created the special look of his wig by strolling back and forth while four courtiers sprayed it with scented powders and fixatives.

Lord Byron was another peacock. His rakishly windblown hair was supposed to look disheveled, as if he gave no attention to it, but just the opposite was true. He set his hair in curlers before bedtime and primped endlessly each morning.

But the Beau changed all that. Restraint in male attire became such a revolutionary new idea that it even elicited a comment from the highbrow English novelist Virginia Woolf: "Without a single noble, important, or valuable action to his credit, he [the Beau] cuts a figure; he stands for a symbol; his ghost walks among us still."

The same could be said for Cary Grant, but with one important exception. Grant, unlike the Beau, had many "noble, important and valuable" actions to his credit—about seventy-two of them, starting with *This Is the Night* in 1932 and ending with *Walk, Don't Run,* in 1966, films that display not only a highly developed personal style but a talent that went beyond mere good looks and fine tailoring.

The irony about Cary Grant as a man of style is that he didn't rely on the personal appearance his fans assume he spent so much time perfecting.

"He didn't depend on his looks," observed George Cukor, who directed him in four films, including *The Philadelphia Story*. "He wasn't a narcissist. He acted as though he was just an ordinary young man and that made him all the more appealing."

Grant might have used skin moisturizers after a session of suntanning; he might have even plucked his eyebrows; but unlike some of his contemporaries, his personal transformation was decidedly low-tech. Novelist W. Somerset Maugham, author of *The Razor's Edge*, had himself injected with animal protein by a Swiss doctor and claimed that the treatments revitalized him. Cary Grant went to no such lengths to maintain his youthful appearance, which makes his ascent to iconic status all the more astounding.

"It was Cary Grant's innate sense of how to be a man that transcended everything else beyond his looks and even what he wore," says Carlo Brandelli. "Obviously the cut of his clothing is incredibly important, and we can talk all day about how elegant we could make somebody look, but if you don't understand intrinsically how to behave as a gentleman, then the finest suits in the world would do very little for you."

Cary Grant was hardly a metrosexual. Cary Grant was the last gentleman, the embodiment of a much higher ideal. He was, as we shall see, a man of great substance as well as great style.

A FRIEND IN NEED

"A true friend is, as it were, a second self."

— CICERO

Cary Grant was one of many celebrities at the 1979 memorial service for Merle Oberon (below), an actress he had known for decades and who had introduced him to his third wife, Betsy Drake, aboard the *Queen Mary* when he was too shy to approach her himself.

Robert Wolders, Oberon's husband, had known Grant since 1972, but they had never been more than acquaintances until the funeral. Wolders says of Grant, "When Merle died I asked him to be a—I hate that word—'pallbearer.' It was an extremely painful experience for me, and at the cemetery after the chapel service, they took the coffin to the grave site, and it all became too much for me, because everybody came up to me and tried to make small talk, saying insignificant things, so I had to move away, and I moved to a little bench some distance away. I think I was sitting with my head down, and suddenly I felt this arm around my shoulder, and it was him. He said, 'This has to be the most painful day of your life, and I hope and pray that there'll never be another one like it,' and I thought that was so perceptive of him. If a very close, close friend had done that, I might not have been surprised, but he more than anyone sensed my pain and what I needed at that point. And then to boot a few days later—I remember it was a Sunday morning—I was in a lot of discomfort. I was just sitting and staring at the walls, and the phone rang, and it was him.

"And again he talked about Merle and about my pain, and I said to him that it's so remarkable that you're calling at this point because this is when I'm at my lowest, and he said that's exactly why I'm calling because I know that."

Wolders then met another friend of Grant's, Audrey Hepburn, his costar in the 1963 film *Charade*, directed by Stanley Donen. Wolders lived with Audrey for the last eleven years of her life.

"He was extremely happy about my relationship with Audrey," says Wolders, "because he was so aware of my pain after losing Merle. I remember him saying something like—and I have to paraphrase it—someone who has been happy with someone once deserves to be happy again with someone else."

Actress Merle Oberon was a close friend of Grant's. When Grant was too shy to approach Betsy Drake, who become his third wife, Oberon introduced them.

Wolders recalls Grant's special brand of sensitivity on another occasion: "One time we ran into him at a Los Angeles hotel, and he was with a few Japanese people, businessmen, I think, and he introduced us. You know how eager people are, especially in this town, maybe not to name-drop but to introduce somebody important, but I remember him saying, even though Audrey and I were not married, he said, 'This is Mr. and Mrs. Wolders,' which I thought was interesting because it meant that our relationship meant more to him than her celebrity."

Wolders sees a parallel between the two Hollywood icons as well as a poignant irony: "He was very much like Audrey, less like Merle. Merle was glamorous, so greatly featured. Audrey was more like Grant; both were intensely private

CG and Audrey Hepburn in 1963's Charade. *"Audrey and I had a wonderful time making* Charade," *said Grant, "and I think it shows."*

people who came to be regarded as the epitome of style and elegance because they had these innate qualities that were so very much focused on in their films that people thought that that was all there was to them. In point of fact, in their daily life, they were extremely down to earth and natural. Certainly with Audrey, and maybe this applies to Grant, too, I think it is because they realized earlier in their careers, early in their lives, that self-worth, self-evaluation based on fame and beauty, is very short lived, so they decided to remain themselves—very realistic, aware, and caring. Cary Grant was an extremely caring and thoughtful man."

SIX

AN INDEPENDENT MAN

"Style is the hallmark of a temperament stamped upon the material at hand." —ANDRÉ MAUROIS

CARY GRANT would no longer be the studio's bitch. It was 1936, his contract with Paramount was up, and he'd had enough.

Gary Cooper was partly to blame. The rangy Midwesterner with the laconic drawl and Lincolnesque facial features was Paramount's main man, the cock of the walk, their top earner, and one of the biggest box-office draws in the world. Cary Grant was strictly second string, forced to settle for the movies Cooper had cast aside or was too busy to make. The year before Grant had starred in *The Last Outpost*, not a bad little film, a macho war story in which he trucked across foreign deserts and fought over the girl with Claude Raines, but it was a Gary Cooper reject. Even more galling, it recycled leftover

CG with style to burn, before he gave up smoking.

footage from *The Lives of a Bengal Lancer*, a Cooper flick. If Grant stayed on, he'd amount to nothing more than a clearinghouse for Cooper's sloppy seconds. And that just wouldn't do, not for Cary Grant, no matter how much money they threw at him.

And Paramount threw a fortune at him. If he signed a seven-year contract, they'd increase his salary from twenty-five hundred to thirty-five hundred dollars a week, a princely sum in those days, especially for a poor boy from Bristol who had no resources of his own, no family support, no financial cushion, nothing but a weekly paycheck on which his entire survival depended.

Moreover, the country was still in the throes of the Great Depression, when there were breadlines in every major city, unemployment was at an all-time high, and a man could live like a king on thirty-five dollars a month.

And he was turning down thirty-five hundred *a week?* It even caused the normally mild-mannered studio boss Adolph "the public is never wrong" Zukor to hurl expletives across the boardroom.

No actor had ever shown such brash self-sufficiency. Not even the studio's biggest stars: Dietrich, Carole Lombard, W. C. Fields, Claudette Colbert, the Marx Brothers, to name just a few. Paramount had made Grant an offer he couldn't refuse—and he went right ahead and refused it. It was a nervy move. Beyond nervy. Especially for an actor who, as Peter Bogdanovich put it, "hadn't really hit it yet."

It was indeed a lot of money, but what Grant wanted was something more than money; he wanted—*demanded*—control over his own destiny, the right to pick and choose his own scripts, because independence was as much a part of the Cary Grant style as fine tailoring and flawless grooming, as ingrained a part of his character as the cleft in his monumental chin. He was, always had been, and always would be an independent man.

IT WAS A TRAIT that had asserted itself early on, when he was a lusty lad of just twelve. Most boys dream of running away to the circus, but Grant, then Archie Leach, actually lived it. He wrote to a clown, Bob Pender, a vaudeville veteran of Drury Lane and leader of an acrobatic act called the Knockabout Comedians, and asked for a job. Pender needed apprentices to fill spots vacated by the young men in his troupe who had been drafted and shipped off to fight in World War I.

An opening was not the problem; Archie's age and lack of parental consent were.

Even as a lad Archie was not the type to let a few "technicalities" stand in his way. So, rather creatively, he lied. In his application to Pender, he swore that he was fourteen, the legal age for leaving school, and forged his father's consenting signature.

Then early one morning, without so much as a by-your-leave to either his father or Augustus Smith, his headmaster at Fairfield Secondary School, he hopped aboard a rumbling milk train at somber Bristol station and caught up with Pender in noisy Norwich, where the Knockabouts were performing.

Lithe, limber, and likeable, Archie tried out for the troupe and was immediately offered a contract. He was paid ten shillings a week; his keep was also covered. Not bad for a lad on the lam who wasn't even a teenager yet. Training as an acrobat was fun, a felicitous release of all that youthful exuberance they'd made him keep pent up at school.

Archie Leach was mighty pleased with himself; his father less so. Elias Leach was perhaps amused by his son's impetuosity, his gumption, the fact that he was quickly becoming a chip off the old block, but Archie was still just an underage runaway who needed to be reined in. Ten days later Elias tracked down his wily son at a theater in Ipswich and hauled him back to Bristol.

"Genius is often an infinite capacity for survival."
— KENNETH ANGER

But Archie would not remain there long.

He was kicked out of school for peeking into the girls' loo. Not that he cared. He was now free of his secondary-school fetters, free at last of its Victorian restraints and restrictions, free to pursue his burgeoning passion for the theater.

His swift departure, however, did not go unnoticed by Fairfield's females. "His expulsion was so unfair," recalled Lillian Pearce, a classmate and one of his earliest admirers. "Several of us girls were in tears over it, because we didn't like to lose him."

He was already a heartthrob, and at such a tender age.

He rejoined Pender as soon as he turned fourteen. Back in his element again, he was never happier. He became a dancer, a tumbler, an acrobat, a stilt walker—mainly a stilt walker—and even played a little barrelhouse piano, skills that would serve him well in Hollywood, still so far in the future that it wasn't even a dream yet.

The troupe promptly lit up the south and west legs of England's vaudeville circuit, performing in Rotherham, Dewsbury, York, Doncaster, Liverpool, Dundee, Eccles, and Morecambe. Tumbling and bumbling, rocking and rolling across the boards, making audiences laugh with his drunken walks, pantomimes, and harlequinades, he was having a great time. He even enjoyed playing the ass end of a dancing cow featured in one silly skit.

He was part of a unit now, a cheerful group of professionals who loved their chosen field as much as he did and were so much more like a family than the troubled one he'd left behind.

"I was so often alone and unsettled at home," he recalled years later, "that I welcomed any occupation that promised activity."

But he was also serious about learning, improving, and slowly evolving into a professional himself.

"At each theatre," he recalled, "I carefully watched the celebrated headline artists from the wings, and grew to respect the diligence it took to acquire such expert timing and unaffected confidence, the amount of effort that resulted in such effortlessness."

Effortlessness. It would become an integral part of the Cary Grant style.

A FEW YEARS LATER, on a bright July day in 1920, the Pender troupe boarded the RMS *Olympic*, sister ship to the ill-fated *Titanic*, and set sail from Southampton to New York City. As they steamed into New York harbor, young Archie caught a glimpse of the Manhattan skyline, a sight he would never forget. Although he could not have known it then, he did realize years later that he had taken the first fateful step toward fulfilling what would become a larger, all-encompassing destiny.

"The most prominent spire in the year of 1920," he recalled, "was the Woolworth Building. If any happy medium, any fortune-telling gypsy, had prophesied I would marry the heiress granddaughter of its founder, no palm would have been crossed with *my* silver."

LEFT
In 1942, Cary Grant married Barbara Hutton, one of America's richest women. The press dubbed the couple "Cash & Cary," a snidely unfair term because it implied that the matrimony was motivated by money rather than love. But Grant by then was financially sound, and Hutton's wealth was protected by an ironclad prenup.
OPPOSITE
CG was the first and only actor able to blend screwball comedy with a sexy stylishness.

The "heiress granddaughter" alluded to was the beautiful but troubled Barbara Hutton, his second wife, a marriage made in 1942 that would incite the press to dub the couple "Cash & Cary," a snidely unfair term because it implied that the matrimony was motivated by loot rather than love. Grant by then was financially sound, and Hutton's wealth was protected by an ironclad prenup.

But that was a long way off.

The Penders were scheduled to perform at the world-famous Hippodrome on Sixth Avenue, between Forty-third and Forty-fourth streets, then the largest theater in the world, with a seating capacity of nearly six thousand. The backstage staff of eight hundred was larger than many of the audiences they'd performed for back in Britain.

The Hippo, as it was aptly called, had a rotating stage a city block long and half a block deep that could hold several hundred performers at once. A constant buzz of activity combined with the immensity of the space made it seem like a world unto itself; it could not have been more unlike the provincial one they'd left behind just eight days before. They would be appearing under the same roof as some of the top acts in the world, even legendary performers like the great Harry Houdini, who wowed audiences by making a ten-thousand-pound elephant named Jennie disappear.

Other big draws were extravaganzas in which sexy girl swimmers and muscular high divers plunged into an understage tank containing 960,000 gallons of water. There was also a quirky cast of dozens of smaller but no less intimidating acts, including zany Joe Jackson, the tramp cyclist; Marceline the clown; Poodles Hannaford, a daring equestrian trickster; and the usual jugglers, sword swallowers, and wacky contortionists who performed on opulent sets amid swirling multicolored lights, cascading waterfalls, and hundreds of high-kicking chorines. Even by today's standards it was a big production—very Las Vegas—one that would make Cirque du Soleil and Mummenschanz pale in comparison.

Archie watched with eyes agog, at once thrilled and, as he characterized it, "petrified." But there was nowhere else he'd rather be: "Today you cannot imagine the size of it. It really was *show* business."

And New York City, in its pre-Depression days, was a jumping Jazz Age Mecca pulsating with the roar of the Roaring Twenties. "The first thing I loved about America was how *fast* it all seemed," Grant recalled.

This monstrous metropolis was the center and the seat of the growing entertainment industry. Vaudeville was at its peak, and a newfangled form of diversion—motion pictures!—was just beginning to catch on, destined to dominate the world of entertainment in the decade to come. There were already one thousand some odd movie theaters in Manhattan alone. No doubt Archie Leach took notice of this new cultural upstart as he rode in the open-air tops of the double-decker buses along fancy Fifth Avenue. He couldn't have overlooked them if he'd tried: the Rivoli and the Roxy, the Paramount and the Loew's State weren't just movie theaters, they were movie *palaces*—soaring structures with floor-to-ceiling marble-and-mirror lobbies that were as big and bustling and brightly lit as a twenty-first-century airport.

The Knockabouts' first gig was a spot in a show called *Good Times*, which ran at the Hippodrome for 455 performances and lasted nine months. Although they appeared on stage only briefly, teetering comically on stilts or executing hilarious pratfalls for about ten minutes in a three-hour show, Archie found it exhilarating and yet another enriching educational experience. He learned how to fit into two well-oiled machines: the Pender troupe and the Hippodrome.

He lived under the same roof with Bob and Margaret Pender, a kind but strict husband-and-wife team, and his fellow performers in a stuffy apartment near Times Square, where everybody pulled his own weight, sharing chores, such as ironing and washing clothes. Archie was given the job of cooking many of the meals (usually a meaty stew), a task he took to cheerfully.

"The first thing I loved about America was how fast it all seemed."

— CG

The Hippodrome was like a large modern-day corporation and required all employees to punch a clock, management's way of keeping track of the seemingly chaotic comings and goings of the numerous acts. Archie was forced to develop a habit of exacting punctuality, both at home and at work. His livelihood would depend on it. There was no dawdling, not even for a callow teenager. Archie toed the line, and punctuality soon became a part of his nature. Even later in life, whether he was on the set of one of his big-budget feature films or at the most casual of social functions, he was never late.

If Archie was homesick, there was very little sign of it, perhaps because the days were long and full, with no time to indulge nostalgic yearnings. After all there was a show to put on. And what a show it was! *Good Times* was a hit, and although the Knockabouts were but a small part of it, the experience was a gratifying one. More important, it led to additional bookings. When the show closed, at the end of April 1921, the Pender troupe hit the road, traveling the American vaudeville circuit and visiting many of the major cities east of the Mississippi.

For Archie it was a wonderful introduction to the exoticism of this immense new country that he would some day make his permanent home.

They kicked off the tour in Washington, DC, doubled back to the Bushwick Theatre in Brooklyn ("What an uncharming place!"); performed at the prestigious Palace Theatre in Manhattan, where they received rave reviews; and then pushed on to Buffalo, Baltimore, Philadelphia, Boston, and across the border to Toronto and Montreal. It was a grueling schedule, but they met many famous figures, including Jack Dempsey, heavyweight boxing champion of the world, and Archie's idol, Harry Langdon, a Chaplinesque clown who had achieved fame in slapstick silent films with such future stars as Joan Crawford.

In mid 1922 the tour ended, and the Pender troupe performed their final show at the Palace, but unlike before, it did not lead to more work. The Pender juggernaut had come to an abrupt halt.

Bob Pender, always a practical man, decided to play it safe. Rather than hack around Manhattan scrounging for employment with many mouths to feed, he thought it would be better to pack up the troupe and return to the mother country, where they could resume a moneymaking tour of the music halls that vied for their accomplished brand of comedy and acrobatics.

It was an eminently sensible idea.

Everybody thought so except one mutinous young man. "Fat chance" (to use one of Grant's favorite phrases) *he'd* go back to dreary rain-soaked Britain. *Noooo* way. He'd hardly scratched the surface of this glittery new world.

So with a few other fellows from the Pender troupe, Archie defected and hatched a plan to remain in Manhattan, yet another manifestation of his fearless independence.

But surely this was a reckless scheme, one that could not possibly succeed. After all he was only eighteen and, unlike Pender, lacked contacts, money, and worldly experience. He was also an Englishman, a foreigner who talked funny. And he had yet to speak one line of dialogue on stage. He was a mere stilt walker. How would he survive?

IN ADDITION TO a wildly independent streak, Grant was also keenly resourceful, supremely self-confident, and even then, gifted with preternatural charm. Years later, looking back on those days, he would remark that it was just the impudence of youth, the product of a cocky kid who "knew that I knew everything."

Which of course he didn't.

But he knew enough to get by. He pocketed the money Pender had given him for his return voyage to England and used it to set up housekeeping in Manhattan, with an eye toward forming a touring troupe of his own.

Pender, no fool, was not pleased. He suspected that he was about to be hoodwinked by the young jackanapes and fired off a letter to Archie's father in Bristol.

"Dear Mr. Leach," he wrote on May 21, 1922, "I am writing to inform you Archie is coming home." Pender hadn't yet figured out Archie's plan, but he had a few choice words about his erstwhile apprentice: "I must tell you he is most extravagant and wants to stay at the best hotels and live altogether beyond his means. He has very big ideas for a boy of his age. . . . He is like all young people. He thinks he only has to ask and have."

Still, Pender didn't want to lose his talented protégé and tried to keep him in his services. First he offered him an increase in salary, the same wage "my daughter and also another of my boys have been getting so I know he could do very nicely on it. . . ."

When that didn't work, he enlisted the help of his wife. "Mrs. Pender has talked to him but it is no use. He will not listen."

Despite Pender's complaints, the tone of the letter is also affectionate, revealing unflagging support and loyalty. "He has been a good boy since he has been with me. . . . So I should like to hear if he arrives home safely. . . . I shall be glad to do anything for him when I return to England."

But Archie had landed in the land of opportunity, and there was no way he would leave it, even if it meant duping the very man who had made it all possible, the father figure who had given him his first break in show business, a warm home, and passage to the very country he refused to depart. Archie felt bad about misleading Pender. He wasn't a cad, just a stubborn and willful young man. As he himself later said, "It must have been very disappointing and difficult for him to leave so many of his boys behind in America, but youth, in its eagerness to drive ahead, seldom recognizes the troubles caused or the debts accrued while passing."

Elegantly stated, but back in 1922 he wasn't at all worried about Bob Pender's hurt feelings; he was more concerned with his own survival. Work on the vaudeville stage was not forthcoming, so he was forced to scramble around for odd jobs, anything that would pay the rent and put food on the table, including a summer stint as a stilt walker at Coney Island, where the local Brooklyn toughs pelted him with rotten tomatoes and winged stones at him. He must've made an enticing target, clomping around on wooden stilts and toting sandwich boards that advertised everything from shoe polish to "50 Attractions for 50 Cents!"

And then there was that suffocatingly hot costume—electric lights crudely attached to his shirt that flashed on and off to draw the attention of the teeming crowds who came to Steeplechase Park to see the circus freaks and fireworks, the merry-go-rounds and magic kingdoms.

A top hat and billowing pinstriped bell-bottoms completed the absurd but eye-catching ensemble. The costume wasn't the worst of it, though. On really bad days, ruffians, just for kicks, knocked him off his perch. They found it entertaining to watch him fall from a height of eighteen feet to the hard pavement below, no doubt hoping he'd break a bone or two, always good for a giggle. It's hard to imagine the elegant Cary Grant in such an inelegant predicament.

Or is it?

At six feet two inches, with the added benefit of an athlete's fit physique, he was indeed a handsome young man, but he was no pushover; he could take the dissing from the local louts. These were lean years for the boy from Bristol, but they instilled in him a toughness that would always inform his trademark elegance, a trait today's actors, as wonderfully appealing as they might be, sorely lack. Gorgeous George Clooney, beautiful Brad Pitt, gentle Jude Law, boyish Orlando Bloom, and other contenders for the throne suffer from a kind of fatal matinee-idol metrosexuality, a visible softness, the result of lifelong cosseting that has cut the heart and soul out of the manly force of their screen presence, if it was ever there to begin with. Grant never lost his edge, the dark side that David Thomson says occasionally "slips into view."

The personification of class, elegance, and a debonair wit was called a "street fighter" by Betsy Drake, to whom he was married from 1949 to 1962. He had class. He had class in spades, but it was the class of an evolved working-class hero, and no amount of foulard silks or tuxedos could ever completely eclipse it.

And we wouldn't want it any other way.

Still, for all of its character-building benefits, the stilt-walking job was a dead end. And he hated it. But he did turn a potential humiliation into a triumph with a simple but significant gesture, one that reveals the substance behind the man of style.

A miserable job it was, but if you saw him at it, as Samuel Marx did, you would never have known he was unhappy. Marx, at one time the head of the Story

Department at MGM, remembered Grant in his stilt-walking days: "This handsome young man was always smiling."

Grant learned this from his mother; she was a woman whose frail appearance, he said, belied her strength.

It also served another equally important purpose; it was a handy survival tool, one he used throughout his career. Betsy Drake explained it this way in a recent interview: "He took me to a preview of a movie, and he said the very important thing is that no matter what people think of the movie or anything, keep smiling. If you show that you're vulnerable, and you show your feelings are hurt, they'll use it against you, and you'll be destroyed, and you mustn't; so keep smiling."

HIS NEXT ODD JOB, however, would make him truly smile . . . a little, anyway. Or at least not groan from soreness and bruises. He met another struggling immigrant, an Australian named John Kelly, who would later find fame as a costume designer at Warner Brothers and win three Academy Awards under the name Orry-Kelly for his work on *An American in Paris, Les Girls,* and *Some Like It Hot.*

The beauty and the beast. CG meets legendary boxer Max Schmeling, known for his classic fights against Joe Louis in the 1930s. Grant eventually lost interest in the sport because of its brutality.

Archie happily hawked Kelly's handsome hand-painted neckties on Sixth Avenue street corners in Greenwich Village. It was a far cry from the Hippodrome, but it was a stage of sorts, a platform for his charm, gift of gab, and winning personality—for what is salesmanship if not a kind of performance?

Archie sold the nifty neckties by the dozens, the proceeds paltry but enough to enable him to remain in America—and that, after all, was the important thing.

But he wouldn't languish long in obscure jobs. Despite his lack of cash, he managed to make the most of his wardrobe, keeping whatever suits he owned carefully cleaned and pressed. His pants might have been a little shiny, his jackets slightly worn, but he discovered that you didn't need a million bucks to look stylish. Style was not a matter of dollars and scents; style was something deeper. For Grant it came from the inside, radiating like a light. It was not the hat so much as how you wore it, as Frank Sinatra put it; and it took him far, to the upper reaches of New York's high society. It wasn't long before the young charmer, barely out of his teens, was making the rounds of the town's cafés and nightclubs where he met the right people, who invited him to fancy dinner parties attended by Henry Ford, Noel Coward, and playboy Jock Whitney.

He was also in demand as an escort, squiring around the opera singer Lucrezia Bori and other luminaries. And that was another thing he loved about America: there was no class system. In Edwardian England you needed inherited wealth, an Etonian education, a posh accent, a title, and lots and lots of land to become a gentleman, assets he most assuredly lacked.

In America, however, the hospitable home of the self-made man, you could create yourself, rise to dizzying heights on your own initiative, become the man you always wanted to be; you weren't limited by accidents of birth or bloodlines.

He was able, then, to move freely among the smart set, something he could never do in patrician-obsessed England, no matter how well one faked being a toff. Although working as an escort did not put much money in his pocket, by making the rounds of these upper-crust New York dinner parties and closely observing the fashionable young men and women who attended them, he added key elements to his inchoate style arsenal—everything from elegant table manners to the art of light banter and pleasant after-dinner conversation. He was still a bit awkward, not yet Cary Grant, but he was definitely headed in the right direction.

HIS DAYS weren't quite as glamorous. He needed to find work, real work, work in the theater, where at least if he broke his neck it would be in front of a large and

ABOVE

Grant, Martha Hyer, and Sophia Loren in a wardrobe test for 1958's Houseboat. *According to famed costume designer Edith Head, Grant liked the color scheme of his wardrobe planned around that of his leading ladies.*

RIGHT

Elegant evening. CG and Martha Hyer on the set of Houseboat.

appreciative audience instead of a gang of street thugs. Adding to the pressure, his stilt-walking job in Coney Island had come to an end; it was now September, and the seasonal fun and games were over. The little cash he had was fast disappearing.

And then there was his dad back in Bristol, who was living with a new woman and their new son. Elias's poorly paying job as a pants presser didn't go very far, so Archie, though struggling himself, generously sent his father whatever he could, often a much-needed couple of quid a week. Quite a responsibility for a young man, but Archie took it in stride; the additional pressure made him work harder and increased his already impressive determination to succeed.

Through the grapevine he heard that R. H. Burnside, the director of the Hippodrome, was planning an extravagant variety show called *Better Times*. It was very much like *Good Times*, the one he'd been in with the Knockabouts. In fact it was something of a sequel. Archie had an idea. And it was a good one. He quickly formed "The Walking Stanleys" with the remaining members of the Pender gang who hadn't returned to England (at least not yet) and sold the act to Burnside. Once again he was back on stage at the Hippodrome, performing pratfalls and somersaults, as well as the inevitable stilt-walking stunts (would he ever get off those damn things? *Soon, soon . . .*).

When the show closed, the Stanleys kept on rolling. They tweaked their act for the Pantages circuit and, in 1924, toured vaudeville houses from Canada all the way to the West Coast, where the twenty-year-old performer got his first taste of the warm Southern California sunshine.

But when the Stanleys returned to New York at the end of the run, the troupe found themselves without further prospects and disbanded; the remaining Pender holdouts, fearing homelessness and starvation, hightailed it back to Britain, but not Archie. Archie remained as stubborn and as determined as ever to succeed.

He found new digs at the National Vaudeville Artists Club, on West Forty-sixth Street, where he was allowed to run up debts while looking for work. Nimble networking landed him a few temporary jobs: he juggled, rode a unicycle, and appeared in a few comedy sketches. He happily filled any spot that was open; whatever skill he lacked, he was happy to learn, even if it meant staying up half the night to do so.

The most memorable gig during this difficult period was with Milton Berle in a variety show that ran at Proctor's Newark Theatre, where he learned how to speak on stage, a scary new realm for the young entertainer whose talent was tumbling, not talking.

But he was a quick study, and he had the best teachers. George Burns and Gracie Allen were also on the bill. From them he learned the all-important comedic skill of timing. Years later George Burns would often quip that "Cary stole my timing but not my cigars."

Then came the fateful meeting with Reginald Hammerstein, younger brother of Oscar Hammerstein II, who suggested, rather out of the blue, that he try musical comedy. It

Katharine Hepburn once described Grant as "a delicious personality who has learned to do certain things marvelously well. He was great fun to act with and laughter reigned around him—a wonderful comedian with an always lively approach to the material."

was a crazy idea. Young Leach was indeed talented, but the only singing he did was in the bath.

Hammerstein had connections, however, and Archie was never one to let an opportunity pass, so he took voice lessons and was apparently good enough for theatrical big shot Arthur Hammerstein to hire him on a "run-of-the-play" basis.

Archie's first role was a bit part as an Australian POW in the musical *Golden Dawn*; he also understudied the lead. The production ran for 184 performances over a six-month period, a propitious start.

Arthur Hammerstein hired him again for another musical comedy, *Polly*, in which he landed the lead role, the one Noel Coward, whose style he emulated, had played to perfection in the London production.

It was a lucky break, but he wasn't quite ready for it. The reviews were uniformly negative. Archie was no Noel Coward, far from it, at least then. "Archie Leach has a strong masculine manner," wrote one critic, "but unfortunately fails to bring out the beauty of the score."

And that wasn't the worst of it.

Archie was summarily fired and replaced. He would learn that a thick skin was just as important to one's survival in show business as comic timing.

But he hardly had the chance to indulge in self-pity, for he soon landed another job. Or so he thought. Marilyn Miller, a popular musical-comedy star of the time, had handpicked him to replace her current leading man in a play called *Rosalie*. There was only one problem. The play was produced by Hammerstein's rival, Florenz Ziegfeld. Not only did Hammerstein spitefully refuse to approve the deal, but he sold Archie's contract to Ziegfeld's rival, J. J. Shubert.

Archie was furious. He had been reduced to a pawn in a feud between two hotheaded swells and missed out on what he perceived to be a great opportunity. But the behind-the-scenes wrangling had taught him yet another show-biz lesson, perhaps the most valuable one of them all: a contract player's destiny is often in the arbitrary hands of businessmen who do not necessarily have the artist's best interest at heart.

Ironically, Archie did well by the Shuberts. Very well indeed. They paid him handsomely and slotted him in a musical called *Boom Boom* with bona fide stage star Jeanette MacDonald. His theatrical ascendancy was remarkably swift for a performer with such little experience—and one who had been recently fired from a major production.

Still, the idea of being "owned" rankled; it lingered in the back of his mind and asserted itself more forcefully when, three years later, in 1931, after being "happily, gainfully, and steadily employed" with a salary that put him on easy street and enabled him to buy a fancy new car, the most luxurious American model on the market, he asked to be released from his contract with the Shuberts.

The Depression was at its height: men were literally begging for work on street corners, and he was walking away from a lucrative relationship. Why?

Hollywood.

It was in the air.

"I think maybe he was the best movie actor that ever was. As opposed to being this monumental star . . . he was a very serious actor."
—ALEXIS SMITH

THE "TALKIES" had arrived—and in a big way. The Depression had made theater tickets a luxury; plays were closing left and right. The movies were the future; everybody said so. Flicks were a far more affordable pastime. Forty million Americans went to the box office every week.

And so did Archie Leach.

All the adventure, all the romance, all the excitement you lack in your daily life are in—Pictures! They take you completely out of yourself into a wonderful new world— Out of the cage of everyday existence! If only for an afternoon or an evening—Escape!

With one difference.

He didn't want to just *go* to the movies; he wanted to be *in* them.

Although he had failed that first screen test at Paramount's New York studio, he was undeterred. The results had been blunt—"bow-legged and neck too thick"—but it didn't stop Archie.

Nothing would.

He sublet his Manhattan apartment, loaded up his posh Packard Sport Phaeton, and headed West for what he called "a vacation."

Just a few short years later, in 1936, after appearing in twenty films under his new name, Cary Grant, he would find himself once again under contract, this time with a big-time Hollywood studio, Paramount Pictures—the very studio that had arranged his first ill-fated screen test. Although he was earning a sizeable salary, he now faced a familiar dilemma: would he sign up for a seven-year hitch, shackle himself to the studio's ball and chain, in return for a plum salary, or would he remain true to himself, strike out on his own as a freelance artist, an unprecedented move back then, one everybody thought was insanely risky?

It was not a difficult decision, not really, for there was only one option for a truly independent man.

FASHIONABLE FURNISHINGS

"Interiors speak!"— VAN DAY TRUEX

ABOVE

CG and "Mr. Smith," the dog, at the piano in
The Awful Truth *(1937). Mr. Smith also appeared
in* The Thin Man *series in the role of "Asta."*

BELOW

*Grant's personal style was present in all areas
of his life—in his home (below), in his office at
Universal Studios (page 122), and even in the
way he traveled (page 123).*

The Cary Grant style was evident in not only
how he dressed but in where he lived and
where he worked.

"Effortlessness is not effortless," says
Kilgour's Brandelli. "It's anything but. However, if
you're naturally interested in how you live in all
areas of your life, and you care fundamentally,
you're going to apply that to every part of your
life—your wardrobe, what you eat, where you live,
the work that you do, that's just a natural thing to
do, isn't it?"

It was for Cary Grant. The decor in his home
was consistent with his sartorial philosophy:
style is elimination. The elegant simplicity of his
Beverly Hills home was noted by *GQ* reporter
Diane K. Shah when she visited him there in
1986 for one of his last interviews.

"In his living room," she wrote, "he is a
gentleman of regal bearing in something very
much like a down-to-earth castle."

The evocation of royalty was particularly apt, for the house, perched on a hilltop with sweeping views of downtown skyscrapers to the east and the Pacific Ocean to the west, followed a design scheme popularized by the Duke of Windsor, one of Grant's earliest stylistic influences. The Duke of Windsor preferred chic white or pastel-hued interiors with colorful accents in his residences to the glittery gilt and gaudy grandeur of the royal palaces; the overall feeling was one of streamlined elegance as opposed to ostentatious luxury, a very modern concept in the 1920s and 1930s, when the duke occupied York House, his London residence, and Fort Belvedere, his weekend retreat.

Grant's hilltop hideaway reflected the same aesthetic. Large windows let in an abundance of light, giving it an airy, cheerful ambiance. A bright green banquette was one of the colorful accents in the white interior that matched the verdant view outside. The hillside sloped down to the crystalline waters of his swimming pool, a further visual refreshment, and orange blossoms, honeysuckle, and white jacaranda bloomed in the garden off the kitchen.

Grant's Hollywood homestead was markedly understated compared to the arduously impressive estates typical of his Bel Air and Beverly Hills compeers, more a sanctuary than a showpiece.

Grant's office on the lot of Universal Studios in the 1950s and 1960s was equally uncluttered. More a comfy den than an austere business space, it was furnished in a combination of manly chocolate brown leather chairs and dark wood paneling brightened by white curtains and a yellow Spanish table trimmed with hand-painted florals.

The trend then was toward Asian design in furnishings, and it can be seen in his choice of framed artwork used as accent pieces amid the traditional tawny baronial comfort.

The exterior also bore his unique stamp. On free afternoons he would retreat to the sundeck that was surrounded by high walls to ensure privacy. Stretched out on a deck chair with his shirt off, he'd relax in the warm rays, touching up his golden tan.

Grant liked to fly in style, too. In 1968, after he retired from films, he became the spokesperson for Faberge Cosmetics, a post he held for sixteen years, and was offered a private jet to facilitate his many appearances around the country. But at that point in his life, he wanted to slow down, not speed up, so the company found an aircraft more to his liking—a somewhat outmoded but slower flying DC3 from the 1930s. The tail dipped to the ground, and it seemed like one of the less-than-stable machines featured in *Only Angels Have Wings*, the 1939 adventure flick about a squabbling team of barnstormers that starred Grant, Jean Arthur, and Rita Hayworth.

That was just what he wanted. In fact he relished the challenge of redecorating the plane's antiquated interior. Mirroring the feeling of his bungalow-cum-office, he used bright yellow armchairs and sofas in tomato red and green to complement the darker woods of the dining table and four burgundy leather swivel chairs.

Although it was something of a flying antique in a jet-set age, it had its fair share of modern conveniences and gadgets, such as a lazy-Susan bar and a tray of liquor bottles that appeared and disappeared with the push of a button.

White curtains trimmed with green tassels hung on picture windows that offered expansive views. The walls of the plane were decorated with family photographs, many of them of his daughter, Jennifer.

He turned the once-scruffy plane into a kind of cozy cottage with wings, a feat of which he was proud. He pointed out to guests its homey comforts, which he considered far superior to the sterile design of modern aircrafts of the day.

And there was music, always music. Whether he was on land or in the air, a piano was never too far out of reach—a spinet at the office, a baby grand at home, and an upright, bolted to the floor of the aircraft, on which he would bang out his old vaudeville favorites, snippets of Dave Brubeck jazz, or Cole Porter tunes.

Grant was a man whose style traveled with him, but he liked to travel light. Wherever he was, he surrounded himself with only a few choice objects—a favorite pair of cuff links, a snapshot of Jennifer, prized pieces of sheet music from the twenties, a small collection of books. His minimalist's pared-down style created a sumptuousness that Thoreau defined as follows: "A man is rich in proportion to the number of things he can afford to let alone."

Grant loved to travel by planes, trains, and automobiles, but his favorite means of transportation was by air, occasionally in a glider.

SEVEN

A WAY WITH WOMEN

"You must have manners of the heart."

—OLEG CASSINI, *IN MY OWN FASHION*

CARY GRANT made good manners sexy.

In 1961 Bob Willoughby was assigned by *Show* magazine (now defunct) to photograph a beautiful New York model named Margo McKendry, who was appearing in her first screen test at Universal-International.

A real stunner, she had the luminous dark looks of Natalie Wood combined with the lithe grace of Mary Tyler Moore, a winning combination that was evident when she walked into the Universal commissary that day and all heads turned.

Even in a setting where beautiful starlets are plentiful and major movie stars are common, she managed to stand out, to command the attention of every alpha male on the premises.

The actor John Saxon would appear in the screen test with her, and George England would direct.

And Cary Grant, the number-one box-office attraction in the world and already an iconic leading man, would read lines with her. Yes, that's right, Cary Grant. Imagine her

"I can't think of him without thinking of him in a beautiful suit, shirt, and tie. I never saw him in jogging clothes or T-shirts; that was such an important part of his image. It was so smart of him. I don't know any other actor who could do that—and I'm not saying it's superficial—it just worked for him in film."

—EVA MARIE SAINT

surprise. A legend of the silver screen was running lines with her, a wide-eyed novice new to Hollywood without a single stage or film credit to her name.

Cary Grant running lines with Margo McKendry in his office at Universal Studios (left). And relaxing with her in the backseat of his Rolls-Royce (above).

"Cary," recalls Willoughby, "was the second person who was confident enough to come over and introduce himself to the new lovely. The actor Howard Keel came over as well but didn't think fast enough, I guess, to offer Margo help with her lines."

Not only did Grant offer to read lines with her, but he invited her back to his office on the Universal lot, where they rehearsed, and later to a more private perch, the back seat of his Rolls Royce.

Judging by the look on her fresh young face in these photos, McKendry is enjoying the experience. In one Willoughby photo she adoringly gazes at Grant as he treats her to one of his trademark grimaces that seems to come right out of the screwball comedies he'd starred in with Katharine Hepburn decades before.

Although fifty-seven, and just five years away from retirement, Grant was in top form that day.

"Probably with the possible exception of Sean Connery," notes Willoughby, "he was the best-preserved actor in films; as he grew older, he still looked marvelous. As to dressing, he was perfection all of the time I saw him."

127

A WAY
WITH WOMEN

But it was more than looks and fine tailoring that made him irresistible. Grant, as McKendry discovered that day, had a way with women.

EVA MARIE SAINT was also treated to Grant's unique brand of charm on the set of *North by Northwest*.

"The first day he said to me, 'Eva Marie, you're going to have such a wonderful time because you don't have to cry in this movie,'" recalls the costar of one of Hitchcock's classiest classics. "I'd done *On the Waterfront, Hatful of Rain*, which had a lot of big emotional and sometimes difficult scenes, and he set the pace that first day, broke the ice, and I thought, 'Oh yeah, I could play a sexy spy lady; what's wrong with that?' He suddenly gave me confidence, and we had so much fun."

She soon discovered that Grant was as sensitive and thoughtful toward others as he was charming.

"I'm very fair-skinned," she says, "and he had that very deep tan, and he had in his contract that the wattage couldn't be over a certain amount because then he would squint, but it had to be pretty bright because of his deep com-

"Hitchcock made everybody in the picture dress in a classic style. . . . He didn't want the picture to date because of the clothes. There's not one outfit I couldn't wear today with a few minor adjustments and not look stylish."
—EVA MARIE SAINT

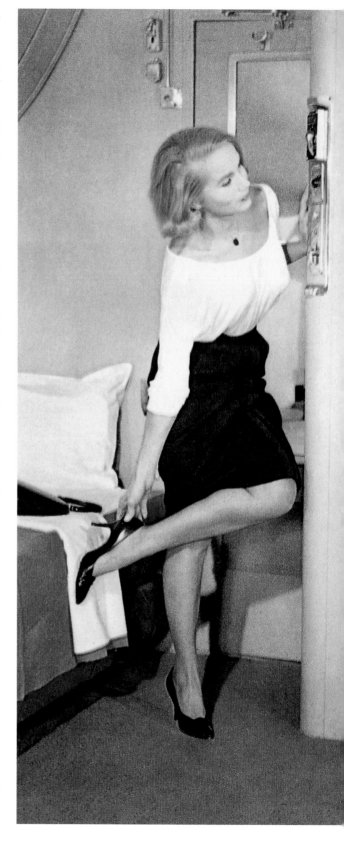

"One surprise after another. Adventurous Cary romanced by the kind of blonde who gets into a man's blood. Even if she has to shoot her way in."

—Trailer for
North by Northwest

plexion. But then one day we were doing a scene, and he saw that I was squinting, and rather than say, 'Eva Marie is having a hard time with that bright light,' he quietly said, 'Wait a minute, could we check the wattage? It's just too bright for me.' And it was so sweet of him."

AUDREY HEPBURN'S first meeting with Grant was equally memorable, but for a slightly more embarrassing reason. They met at a Paris bistro before shooting began on the 1963 film *Charade*; it would become the site of one of Hollywood's most famous mishaps.

"As it was early Spring," recalled Hepburn, "Cary, who was always dressed impeccably, was wearing an exquisite light tan suit. I know I was thrilled to meet him, and I must have been terribly excited, because not ten seconds after we started chatting I made some gesture with my hand and managed to knock an entire bottle of red wine all over poor Cary and his beautiful suit."

Audrey, of course, was horrified. "Here we'd only been just introduced!" she said. "If I somehow could have managed to crawl under the table and escape without ever having to see him again, I happily would have."

Grant, however, remained unruffled, in much the same way he does in *Charade* when Audrey's ice-cream cone topples onto his lapel as they stroll along the Seine.

Grant casually removed his wine-soaked jacket and "pretended, very convincingly," remembered Audrey, "that the stain would simply go away."

But Grant's chivalrous gesture was hardly enough to assuage Audrey's embarrassment.

"Oh, she was still mortified," says Rob Wolders. "And Grant knew that she would be—that's the kind of man he was—so the next day he sent her a tin of caviar to her hotel suite, with a charming little note that said please don't worry about the suit."

Audrey's fears—and embarrassment—were finally allayed, and the two not only developed an affection for each other that shows on-screen, but they were good friends long after the movie wrapped.

GRANT'S WAY WITH women offscreen was markedly different from the way his romantic relationships were depicted on film. In real life he preferred younger women, pursued them almost exclusively, and quite aggressively; even married a few of them.

A poster for Charade *with Cary Grant and Audrey Hepburn.*

But on-screen he was reserved, almost sexually aloof, diffident, not at all the sexual aggressor.

And for a very good reason.

"He was worried," according to director Peter Bogdanovich, "about seeming like a dirty old man."

But he needn't have been. The public still wanted to see him with young, sexy, glamorous women, even if he was old enough to be their father.

The solution to Grant's discomfort was a deceptively simple one: he would let his leading ladies chase him.

And it worked remarkably well, creating a more sophisticated kind of sexual tension than was common in the fifties, when cinematic tastes were changing from "glamour to grit, from romance to realism," toward, as Grant himself put it, "the blue jeans, the dope addicts, the Method." Movie audiences were eating up Brando for breakfast, digging the way-cool James Dean, and gleefully gasping at the pelvic gyrations of Elvis Presley. The antihero was the hep new thing. The suave leading man was old news, strictly Dullsville.

Or was he?

Some of Grant's most memorable films were made in the fifties, many of them classics—*To Catch a Thief* (1955), with Grace Kelly; *An Affair to Remember* (1957), with Deborah Kerr; *Indiscreet* (1958), with Ingrid Bergman; *Houseboat* (1958), with Sophia Loren; *North by Northwest* (1959), with Eva Marie Saint; and *Operation Petticoat* (1959), his highest-grossing film ever.

Perhaps it is a testament to the democratic tastes of American popular culture that it could celebrate two diverse aesthetics at the same time.

Still, Grant wasn't taking any chances. In 1962, when he was offered the lead in *Charade* opposite the much younger Audrey Hepburn, he insisted that the script be changed so that he wouldn't seem like a leering, albeit distinguished-looking, old codger hustling a pretty young thing half his age.

"He made me change the dynamic of the characters and make Audrey the aggressor," explained Peter Stone, who wrote the screenplay. "She chased him, and he tried to dissuade her. She pursued him and sat in his lap. She found him irresistible, and ultimately he was worn down by her."

The result was a perfect pairing. The sparkling dialogue, spiced with witty double entendres, was expertly handled by two pros who crackled with on-screen chemistry, despite the age gap, or maybe because of it:

> Reggie (Hepburn): Won't you come in for a minute?
>
> Peter (Grant): No, thank you.
>
> Reggie: I don't bite, you know. Unless it's called for.
>
> Peter: How would you like a spanking?
>
> Reggie: How would you like a punch in the nose? Quit treating me like a child.
>
> Peter: Well, then, stop behaving like one.

PORTRAYING THE RELATIONSHIP between Grant and Hepburn with a naughty suggestiveness proved far more erotic than straightforward up-against-the-wall sexual roughhousing ever could, at least for some audiences. It was, as film critic Pauline Kael termed it, "sex with civilized grace, sex with mystery."

It was a formula that had worked well in other Grant vehicles, particularly a few years earlier in Hitchcock's *To Catch a Thief*, in which Grant plays John "the Cat" Robie, a jewel thief who, while lounging around the French Riviera in stylish silk threads and loafers, meets Frances "Francie" Stevens, a willful and wily American oil heiress played by the much younger Grace Kelly. Grant was fifty-one; she was twenty-five.

But she was actually the "older woman" in a tricky triangulation that included the sexy young French actress Brigitte Auber, who plays Danielle, Frances's rival for Grant's affections. Danielle, we are told, is "barely out of her teens."

In one scene they meet while swimming in the Mediterranean, and the two women quickly bare their claws. Francie and Danielle exchange bitchy barbs, all age related, while Grant looks on, amused by the catfight.

> Robie: Say something nice to her, Danielle.
>
> Danielle: She looks a lot older up close.
>
> Francie: To a mere child anything over twenty might seem old.
>
> Danielle: A child? Should we stand in shallower water and discuss it?

HITCHCOCK AND GRANT were on the same page about the age thing, so they had the young Danielle and the soon-to-be Princess Grace make all the moves, some rather bold, as in one early scene when Grant escorts glittering Grace back to her room. Although he's obviously attracted to her—what man wouldn't be?—he behaves like a perfect gentleman, keeping whatever feelings he has for her well hidden. Perhaps a little too well hidden: his lack of demonstrable ardor irks the poor little rich girl, who is used to getting what she wants. *And she wants him.*

But she, too, remains equally cool and circumspect. Until, that is, she opens the door to her suite. She turns, looks brazenly into his eyes and moves in for the kill, kissing him passionately on the mouth. She then retreats, having made her unequivocal point, and smiles coyly as she teasingly shuts the door in his face. "It's as though," Hitchcock remarked, "she'd unzipped Cary's fly."

To Catch a Thief was a huge hit. And a good thing, too, because if it had flopped, it might have spelled the end of Grant's career, and classics like *North by Northwest* would never have been made, at least not with Grant. The public would never regard a Cary Grant movie, even a mediocre one, with indifference; there would always be an audience for his films. But he would have pulled the plug himself, as he had done in November of 1952, when he shocked the world by announcing, rather suddenly, that he was retiring from the motion-picture industry.

The reason? He thought he was too old to be a leading man. Cary Grant, at forty-eight, too old? He was as sleek and lean as the thoroughbreds he was fond of watching run at the Hollywood Park Racetrack.

But he did not see himself as others saw him. He just wasn't sure how he would hold up under the scrutiny of the new high-clarity VistaVision process, Paramount's answer to CinemaScope, the newfangled wide-screen technology boasted about by rival studios.

There were other reasons too. He had already climbed onto the pantheon of cinematic greats. Already a wealthy man, he didn't need the money. Thanks to decades of high earnings and shrewd investing, he was one of the richest movie stars in the world. In 1947 his wealth had been estimated to be about a

Author Donald Spoto met Grant in 1979 at the Beverly Hilton Hotel, where Alfred Hitchcock was presented with a Lifetime Achievement Award. "The only difference," Spoto says, "was that in his on-screen persona he rarely laughed out loud or had big emotional scenes; everything was downplayed. But that night he was gracious, he was warm. I was two tables away from him, and I looked over at Hitch, who was as indecipherable as always, and Cary was next to him laughing and enjoying himself. It was just thrilling to meet Grant. I didn't see any difference that night between him on-screen and off except that he was more animated. I just saw a charming and witty man."

billion dollars in today's currency. So why risk an anticlimactic return? Or worse, an all-out flop, a blemish on a near-perfect career? After three decades of non-stop work, during which he completed sixty films, sometimes as many as six in one year, it was time to quit and do all the things a demanding career had prevented him from doing, like spend time with his wife, Betsy, and travel. He loved to travel. According to Gregory Peck, "He had great curiosity. He was also interested in the news, politics, and in meeting new people."

He read books and relaxed, touched up his tan, and generally enjoyed the fruits of his considerable labors. Charitable works were also on the agenda. In

ABOVE

Hitchcock instructed the props department to make the cups three feet high, so that when he pulled the camera back, both the cup and Ingrid Bergman looked especially sharp and dramatic.

OPPOSITE

Cary Grant and Ingrid Bergman in Notorious *(1946).*

OPPOSITE

"When I made That Touch of Mink *with Doris Day (left) I took her to certain fashion houses that I knew had the type of dress a girl could afford. Remember, she played a secretary. I took her to Anne Klein, who had a range of clothes, very reasonable."*

— CG

"He looks into your eyes, not into your forehead or your hair, as some people do. He can make love to me on the screen when he's ninety."

— DORIS DAY ON CG

TOP

Cary Grant with Suzy Parker, who some say was the first supermodel.

ABOVE

Movita, CG, and Deborah Kerr on the set of 1953's Dream Wife. *"From Archie Leach to Cary Grant. What a giant step. And yet he became Cary Grant. He really became him."*

— DEBORAH KERR

An affair between CG and sexy Sophia Loren during the filming of The Pride and the Passion *(1957) resulted in tension on the set of* Houseboat *(right). Director Melville Shavelson: "Cary agreed to go through with the film feeling that if he did he might have a chance of getting back with Sophia. He tried and the only way she finally got rid of him was to marry Carlo Ponte.*

"We had the scene where he was supposed to be dancing with Sophia in the nightclub. What came through for me of course was the battle that was going on between the two of them at the moment, but it didn't matter because the audience interpreted it as love."

1953 he and Betsy sailed to Asia, where they visited hospitals that cared for wounded Korean War veterans.

Still, the scripts poured in. There was more of a demand for his services than ever. During this period he turned down some classics, including *Guys and Dolls*, *The Bridge on the River Kwai*, *Sabrina*, and *A Star Is Born*, but he didn't care. He was tired of making films, tired of the behind-the-scenes wrangling involved in big-budget features. He was doing just fine away from the bright lights, the prying public eye.

That was until Hitchcock stalked him with a draft of *To Catch a Thief*, the story of a retired jewel thief, who like the actor, might not be so retired after all.

"My real name is John Robie. I haven't stolen a piece of jewelry in fifteen years. The police won't believe me, but they're chasing the wrong man!"

GRANT TRIED to put Hitch off, as he had been doing for the previous two years, but the director seemed to know Grant better than Grant knew himself.

"There isn't a thing wrong with you, old man," said Hitchcock, flushed with the recent commercial and critical success of *Rear Window*, "that a first-rate screenplay won't cure."

"Don't count on it, Hitch," replied the shrewdly elusive veteran film star.

But in early 1954 Hitchcock, undeterred, drove from Los Angeles to Grant's Palm Springs hideaway, where they chatted while having lunch by the swimming pool, munching on turkey tea sandwiches served British style, with the crusts cut off and sliced into elegant diamond shapes.

It was a hot day, bright and sunny, not a cloud in the azure sky. Banana and palm trees offered privacy and shade from the hot desert sun. The water in the pool was refreshingly cool and crystalline. Grant, radiantly tanned from riding horses in the canyons of Cowles Mountain, was upbeat and relaxed. Even his dress reflected his new lifestyle. Instead of the usual gray banker suit or bespoke blazers, he wore an embroidered Western shirt and denim jacket, but even these run-of-the-mill cowboy clothes bore his distinctive stamp. The jacket had a special cut with double-pointed or "sawtooth" pocket flaps, and the dull metallic snaps were replaced with pearl. Even his jeans were custom made by "the kind folks at Levi's," who cut them higher in the rise for greater comfort and fit.

Go back to work? Why? What for?

But Hitchcock kept at him. Grant hemmed and hawed. Although he still

looked great, his concerns about a comeback—the word *Grant and Brigitte* all actors dislike—were valid. None of his movies had ever *Auber on the set of* To lost money, but his last few outings hadn't been smash Catch a Thief *(1955).* hits. Commercial success was important to him. He might have been indifferent to critical reviews, good or bad, but he cared deeply about what the public thought, wanted, and paid to see. *People Will Talk* (1951), with Jeanne Crain, in which he played a kind of New Age doctor with a Deepak Chopra bedside manner, dealt with serious themes: an attempted suicide, an out-of-wedlock pregnancy, a spiritual healing.

But it was not a success, so he returned to light comedy, attempting to deliver what he thought the public wanted. *Room for One More* (1952), with Betsy Drake, and *Monkey Business* (1952), with Ginger Rogers and busty new-comer Marilyn Monroe, didn't fare much better. They'd trotted out the screwball-comedy formula that had made him a star in the 1930s, but to postwar audiences it seemed redundant, a little corny, and lacking in the spark that had charged the earlier films.

But he never blamed the producer, the director, or the screenwriter. He blamed himself, concluding that audiences were tired of *him.*

"Cary was very vulnerable to criticism," said Bogdanovich. "He'd had a few flops and I think he wasn't happy with the pictures he'd made and that maybe the public didn't want him anymore."

Finally Hitchcock convinced him otherwise. It was a great script, for starters, but there were two other elements that pushed Grant off the fence: Grace Kelly and location shooting in the south of France, a scenic paradise. And the food wasn't bad either.

Although she was a relative newcomer, the striking young actress who would later become the Princess of Monaco was greatly admired by Grant. He had been very impressed with what he had seen of her in *Dial "M" For Murder* and *Rear Window* (both 1954), two classic Hitchcock thrillers.

Grace Kelly turned out to be his ideal leading lady; Hitchcock's too: elegant with a touch of icy reserve, demure but also feisty when she had to be; ladylike, soigné, well mannered, and a seasoned pro who, though with only a few feature films to her credit, had cut her teeth on countless soap operas and live television

"Grace," says Donald Spoto, author of The Art of Alfred Hitchcock, *"said something to me that was so honest and ingenuous that you could never accuse Grace of vanity about it. She said, 'You know, on a plane recently they showed* To Catch a Thief, *and I was watching,' and she said 'Cary and I were so beautiful.' Well, it's true, and she would have been a fool to deny it or not see it. She said we had such fun, and they did. They were great friends. I think that's a charming story from Grace, and I think it has the context of great appreciation and great affection and great gratitude for having done that film. It's not about her vanity at all. And I said to her, 'Grace,' who was forty-six when she said that to me, 'What do you mean "were"?' She wasn't one of these actresses who never looked at her films, that can't bear to see themselves. She loved it. She appreciated it."*

shows where she'd honed improvisational skills that enabled her to keep up with an old pro like Grant.

Grant also admired her intelligence. "She had the most incredible ESP about me," he said. "She could almost read my thoughts. She was cool and reserved, and then she'd say something about my own mood or attitude and it was like she was completely tuned in."

And Hitchcock was his ideal director: "Hitch and I had a rapport and understanding deeper than words. . . . He was so incredibly well prepared. I never knew anyone as capable. He was a tasteful, intelligent, decent, and patient man who knew the actor's business as well as he knew his own."

So what more could Grant want?

"Cary was very vulnerable to criticism," said Bogdanovich. "He'd had a few flops and I think he wasn't happy with the pictures he'd made and that maybe the public didn't want him anymore."

Money? Perhaps. Never shy about demanding top dollar for his services, he asked for the sky. Studio execs said forget it; let's get Jimmy Stewart, a top box-office draw who would work for less. Hitchcock thought Stewart was a marvelous actor but too old for the part. An odd objection, considering that Stewart was four years younger than Grant. The truth was Jimmy Stewart just *seemed* older. In any case Hitch wanted Grant, and he wanted him desperately, for he knew this was a Cary Grant role and no one, not even the talented Mr. Stewart, could do Cary Grant better than Cary Grant.

Hitch would do anything to get Grant on board, even if some of the star's compensation had to come out of his own pocket.

And it did.

But it would be worth it. The droll director, whose television show *Alfred Hitchcock Presents* had by then made him a world-famous celebrity in his own right, gladly ponied up.

According to Hitchcock biographer Patrick McGilligan, Hitch "would get his usual 10 percent of the film, but only after the studio had subtracted Grant's 10 percent from the gross."

It was only money, after all. The important thing was to get Cary Grant in the picture.

So the deal was done.

And suddenly, after a two-year hiatus, Cary Grant was eager to return to work.

Filming commenced in April, and it was a happy production. "I always went to work whistling," Grant recalled.

And it shows on-screen. Both stars were full of fun and mischief, relaxed enough with each other to improvise scenes that made the picture only better, as in the famous bluff-top picnic sequence that overlooks the travel-folder heaven of Monte Carlo.

"Do you want a leg or a breast?" asks Francie, with a wry smile, dipping into the wicker picnic basket. Robie, with one of those priceless Cary Grant looks, replies, "You make the choice."

It was an ad-lib, the result of Grant and Kelly's relaxed, cheerful, and somewhat silly mood that day. "They carried on the fun," according to Hitchcock friend and film critic John Russell Taylor, "even after Hitchcock yelled cut!"

Grant also got on well with the rest of the cast. Between takes he did the mambo in Brigitte Auber's trailer. Betsy visited him on the set, and they enjoyed lavish dinner parties hosted by Hitchcock and his wife, Alma, with Grace Kelly and Oleg Cassini.

GRANT'S COURTLY CHARM and general consideration of others endeared him to the crew as well as the cast.

Sylvette Baudrot, who was in charge of continuity, fondly recalled working with the dashing star while on location. She had helped him with some tricky French dialogue in a key scene for which Grant was grateful. After filming in France was completed, she found a note from him stuck in the door of her room at the Carlton Hotel, where the cast and crew were staying. She recalled, "I had this letter in my keyhole, and he wrote, 'Dear Sylvette: Alas, I leave in a hurry without opportunity to get you a little present of remembrance and appreciation, so instead please be a dear and get yourself something you may prefer. You have my happiest thoughts and gratitude. Au revoir, Cary Grant.' There was French money in the envelope and I bought myself something that, as he said, 'I might prefer'—a striped shirt just like the one he wore in the movie!"

"No one else looked so good and so intelligent at the same time."
— DAVID THOMSON

GRANT LIKED to rewrite scenes, change dialogue, and fiddle about with camera angles, a predilection that was sometimes, but not always, welcomed by the master of suspense.

"Hitch didn't want to make changes while on the set, so he would palm Grant off to John Michael Hayes, the screenwriter," explained Steven DeRosa, author of *Writing with Hitchcock*, "but he had told Hayes to delay him. 'I don't want to make any changes right now. Delay him until it's too late and we'll have to shoot the scenes as is.'

"Cary Grant knew he was being put off, but he was gracious about it, until one day he felt strongly about a scene and went to Hitch and said can we please try it my way once and then we'll try it your way. Hitch agreed, but when it came time to shoot the scene, he saw the opportunity to play a joke on his favorite leading man.

"He whispered to the crew that they were going to shoot the scene both ways, but after they shot it Hitch's way, they were instructed to burst into applause.

"And they did. Cary Grant looked flustered and said, 'Well, Hitch, I guess we'll do it your way.' Later on he told Grant that he had primed the crew. Grant enjoyed the gag as much as everybody else had."

TO CATCH A THIEF is a stylish comedy with some action-hero moments, but the clothes worn by its stars are as entertaining as the story line. Famed costumer Edith Head, one of Hitch's favorites, handled the habiliments. Most of them anyway. Hitchcock gave her full leeway with Grace Kelly's gorgeous gowns but told her not to mess with Cary's clothes.

Hitch trusted Grant to select his own wardrobe. "If he wanted me to wear something very specific he would tell me," said Grant, "but generally I wore simple, tasteful clothes—the same kind of clothes I wear off screen."

Like the dark brown leather loafers hand made for him by Maxwell's on Dover Street in London.

Or the elegant tuxedo he wears to the casino, a garment that seems to glisten as if it had been constructed out of diamond threads. He wears it with a faultlessly white shirt that also glows as if it's piped with halogen illumination.

We have, of course, seen him in a tuxedo before. We *expect* to see him in a tuxedo; it's a CG trademark, like Superman's cape.

But it's the striped pullover with the jaunty red foulard worn around his neck that is the real eye-catcher, the real surprise.

The pullover, however, wasn't his first choice. Grant showed up on the first day of shooting in one of his prized button-down shirts, but Sylvette Baudrot

vetoed it because it was too modern for the time period of the film. So Grant went shopping, happily scouring local boutiques, trying on a multitude of "looks." None seemed right until he came upon the striped shirt and red silk scarf. They were a unique but perfect pairing, both for Grant and for the film's time period. It sets him apart sartorially, imbuing him with a suitably rakish air. There's something that spells danger about that foulard, as if he's hiding something (which he is). The pullover also flatters his trim physique without being flashy, and it fits the shady nature of John Robie.

Stripes, especially horizontal stripes, vibrate on-screen. Costume designers usually eliminate them from the wardrobe for this very reason. But they're mesmerizing on Grant, even a little dizzying if you stare at them too long, an effect that is right in step with the character he plays: they keep you slightly off balance.

Grace Kelly is his sartorial equal. She glides through her scenes in a rustle of floor-length chiffon evening gowns that would trip up a veteran runway model.

"Hitch and I had a rapport and understanding deeper than words. . . . He was so incredibly well prepared. I never knew anyone as capable. He was a tasteful, intelligent, decent, and patient man who knew the actor's business as well as he knew his own." —CG

The first one is powder blue, the second one pearly white, and the last one a gold lamé dazzler, all three similarly designed to reveal her sensuous shoulders and creamy, swanlike neck—a neck that would drive a vampire out of his mind.

Her most memorable outfit, however, is a swimsuit ensemble, an eye-popping black-and-white number accessorized with an arresting Flying Nun hat, not exactly an outfit you'd see in the Hamptons. While most females would bare flesh to seduce a man, she's almost completely covered, proving that you can dress to kill even if you're going to the beach.

Clothes to make the man, so to speak.

HITCHCOCK AND his screenwriters rewrote some of their dialogue to make it more suggestive, expecting it to be censored. The Hays office, that weird watchdog of public morality, was still in business at the time, breathing down his neck every step of the way, forcing him to trim or cut any scene with even the slightest salacious buzz. But the censors, apparently, were either asleep at the wheel or too busy ogling Grace Kelly to notice the spicy dialogue. For the most part they voiced very few objections.

In the famous fireworks scene, the cat-and-mouse game between Robie and Francie comes to an end. Sparks fly, literally and figuratively. Of course it's flirty Francie who is the aggressor.

Frances: If you really want to see the fireworks, it's better with the lights off. I have a feeling that tonight you're going to see one of the Riviera's most fascinating sights. *(Robie is caught glancing at her strapless evening gown.)* I was talking about the fireworks . . .

Robie: May I have a brandy? Would you care for one?

Frances: Some nights a person doesn't need to drink. . . . Give up, John. Admit who you are. Even in this light I can tell where your eyes are looking. *(Close-up of her necklace and generous décolletage.)* Look. Hold them! *Diamonds*—the only thing in the world you can't resist. *(Fireworks explode in the background as she kisses his fingers one by one, and places his hand beneath the necklace.)* Ever had a better offer in your whole life? One with everything? . . . Just as long you're satisfied. *(Fireworks explode again.)*

Robie: You know as well as I do this necklace is imitation.

Frances: Well, *I'm* not. *(They kiss. Cut to the climax of the fireworks display.)*

THE RELATIONSHIP IS consummated, off camera of course. No grunting and groping here. What we see instead are the orgasmic bursts of Roman candles and other pyrotechnics symbolically soaring across a darkened sky, framed beautifully by the balcony window. It's a classic Hitchcock moment, one celebrated for its tasteful and witty depiction of sexual efflorescence as much as it is for its erotic charge, an erotic charge that still works its magic on jaded seen-it-all audiences of today. And the reason is because it has style. Style to burn.

Even Frances's wealthy mother, played by Jessie Royce Landis, is sex obsessed. Upon seeing the dapper Grant for the first time, she smacks her lips and says, *"Yum.* I wouldn't mind buying that for you, dear." It's a line that could have come right out of *Sex and the City.*

Francie, though dressed in a prim pink dress, has a naughty mind to equal her mother's. She says to Robie, who is pretending to be a lumber-industry tycoon, "The big handsome lumberman from America. I'll bet you told her all of your trees are sequoias."

When she finally surrenders to his unique charm, she says that it looks like "the cat has a new kitten."

Earlier, when they're sparring verbally, he says she needs "something I have neither the time nor the inclination to give you: two weeks with a good man in Niagara Falls."

THE FILM WRAPPED in September of 1954, and everybody was thrilled with the result. Even normally nervous studio executives were confident that it would do well. Grant, however, wasn't so sure.

Ever wary, he was a man who kept his own counsel and would not rejoice until he heard from the only critics who mattered to him: the ticket buyers. In fact he would not take on another project for more than a year, until he was sure that this latest venture was exactly what the public wanted.

Again, he needn't have worried.

Not only did he hold up well in the sharp-eyed VistaVision cameras, but clearly age had made him more drop-dead gorgeous than ever. "Everyone," wrote one critic, "was talking about how great he looked."

This was not a new Cary Grant, not a "reinvented" Cary Grant, but the perfection of the Cary Grant persona that had long been in the making, an iconic image that had reached its apogee, ironically, at a time when its creator thought it had lost its luster.

"... he said his secret was that he was never quite in fashion; he never went by the fads. He never went by what's in this year. The things that he wore were the classic line. And he knew what looked good on him and he'd talk about less is more when he would travel; he would travel with very little ..."

—EVA MARIE SAINT

"No one else looked so good and so intelligent at the same time," wrote film critic David Thomson.

Although not all reviews were positive—another critic wrote, "The dialogue is so bad that Cary looks embarrassed to be saying it"—the film garnered several Academy Award nominations. Edith Head was nominated for best costume design. Although she lost to Charles Le Maire for *Love Is a Many Splendored Thing*, Robert Burk won for his VistaVision cinematography.

In New York crowds mobbed Radio City Music Hall on opening day. *To Catch a Thief* was a major box-office smash that year, and reviewers praised not only the film but also singled out its male star's nuanced performance. Film critic and author Richard Schickel said that Grant seemed "to glow, to radiate masculine power perfectly deployed ... so casual, yet so commanding ... the only permissible response to him is bedazzlement."

Finally, with all of his doubts assuaged, Grant was back—and better than ever.

Ironically, the age thing that he thought was a liability had turned out to be a great asset. Pauline Kael wrote that age had not just "purified" his looks, but that it had also purified his acting: "His romantic glamour, which had reached a peak in 1939 in *Only Angels Have Wings*, wasn't lost: his glamour was now a matter of his resonances from the past, and he wore it like a mantle."

Still, the girl would always chase him in future films. And the endings would always be happy. Offscreen, however, he was not so fortunate. Unlike in the movies, there were no happy endings.

Except one.

Cary Grant and Jessie Royce Landis in North by Northwest.

Tall, Dark, and Very, Very Tan

CG maintained a tan because he liked its "healthful appearance."

Cary Grant's golden tan was as much a part of his iconic persona as his sartorial eloquence; but was it real?

"It's real," says director and author Peter Bogdanovich.

But in some films, such as *Houseboat*, it doesn't look real. "It's just hard to tell," he explains, "because of the kind of screen or monitor you're watching him on."

Makeup artist Ben Lane, who is now retired and living in Palm Springs, agrees. "It was real," he says. "I worked with him on a lot of movies, including *Gunga Din*, in 1939, and his last movie, *Walk, Don't Run*, which came out in 1966. He was always very tan. It became a problem in the early days because he was so dark and Katharine Hepburn was so light skinned; it made it seem like he was a black hole next to a glowing orb. The lighting guys had a terrible time."

But if Cary Grant didn't use makeup, what would a makeup artist do on a Cary Grant set?

"Well," says Lane, "I did other things. I cut his hair. He knew exactly what he wanted. He was very easy. We always got on well."

What about rainy days? What did Cary Grant do on rainy days to maintain his trademark tan?

"I don't know," says Lane. "I didn't follow him around. Maybe he used a sunlamp. A lot of the stars used sunlamps."

It seems likely. Even early in Grant's career, his tan was a subject that caused Hollywood reporters like Sidney Skolsky to speculate about its origins. Skolsky addressed it in Tintypes, a popular column that appeared in the 1930s. "Archie Leach," he wrote, "has a mania for becoming browned, oh! Pardon me! Tanned, as he can never get enough of good old Sol. This weakness he inherited from boyhood when his pater gave it to him good. Usually has some portable tan-making device in his lodgings so that when the mood strikes him, he can turn it on and give himself some esthetic rays on his old corpus. . . ."

Years later it was still a viable subject for media mavens. "Like most transplanted Englanders," wrote Jan Vantol in an article entitled "Introducing Your Heart's Desire," "he has turned sun worshipper and delights in spending hours asleep in his patio, basking in the hot California sunshine."

Eva Marie Saint, Grant's costar in the Hitchcock classic *North by Northwest*, thinks that perhaps Grant's reputed sun worship was a myth. "Knowing what we know now about skin cancer," she says, "I hope it wasn't real. His skin would have turned to leather. I think he used a stain. Or makeup."

Leslie Caron, Grant's costar in *Father Goose* (1964), sees no reason to think that Grant's

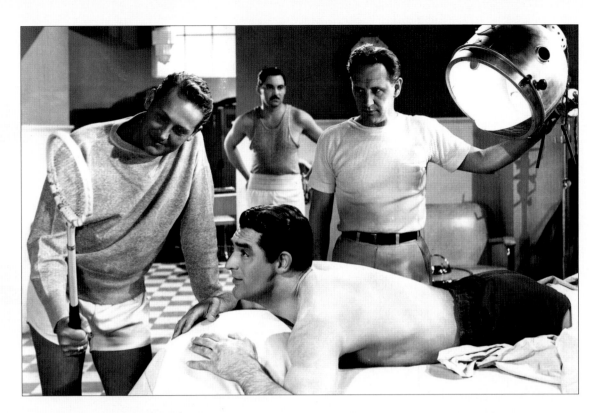

sunny glow wasn't natural. "Cary was dark-skinned naturally and took the sun very well."

And neither does Svend Petersen of the Beverly Hills Hotel, a favorite haunt of Grant's, where he often lunched at the Polo lounge. "He was tan," says Petersen. "Even after he retired he always dressed beautifully and had a beautiful tan. It wasn't one of those orange-type tans."

And Petersen should know. Before joining the hotel's public relations team as hotel ambassador, he worked as the manager of the pool and cabana, for which he was nicknamed the "Poolside Prince." It was a job he held for more than thirty years, beginning in 1959, and one that brought him into contact with hundreds of stars, from Burt Lancaster to Britney Spears. He even gave some of them swimming lessons. For Faye Dunaway's turn as Joan Crawford in the 1981 movie *Mommie Dearest* ("No wire hangers!"), Petersen taught Dunaway the style of stroke popular in

"Come on, Hank. Get that sunlamp ready . . . fifteen minutes, nothing. I gotta get a deep Florida tan if it takes all afternoon."
—CG IN THE AWFUL TRUTH

the 1940s so that she could portray Crawford authentically, even when she was in the water.

"You could see the tan lines around his neck from where the flesh folded," says Petersen, "so that's how you can tell it was real."

Grant himself said that he didn't like the brush-on tanning gels popular in his day. "They look artificial," he said.

"Perhaps," says Eva Marie Saint, "he used a combination of all three—natural sun, a sunlamp, and a bit of stain or makeup for touch-ups? He knew what looked good on him. He was a very clever man."

It's a mystery that will no doubt go unsolved. And maybe that's the way it should be. After all, even an icon should be allowed some secrets.

157

EIGHT

ROMANTIC HEART

"In spite of age, one can still escape into the romantic."
—BEATRICE WOOD

I N THIS CANDID PHOTOGRAPH taken in the early 1980s, Cary Grant and his wife, Barbara, stand together, a united front against a prying world. It says a lot about their relationship. Take, for instance, the way they're holding hands; the grasp is a mixture of both strength and tenderness, an equality of emotion in spite of the forty-six-year age difference.

It's a fine autumn day, clear and bright, a little glaring. Barbara is wearing sunglasses and stands slightly out front, as if offering herself as a shield to the intrusion of the camera on what was a private moment.

The camera, of course, was ever present in Grant's life, a device that is responsible for his enduring fame but also his loss of privacy, the Faustian bargain all movie stars make, whether wittingly or unwittingly. The camera was now a part of Barbara's life, too.

But both are smiling, as if in acceptance of notoriety's downside, of being in the spotlight when they didn't particularly want to be. Graciousness, perhaps, was a gentle yet powerful means they used to combat the invasion, a way of enabling them to retain their dignity, composure, and ease.

CG with wife Barbara. They were married from 1981 until his death in November 1986.

Grant had struggled with the privacy issue his entire life and, by his own admission, felt he wasn't as patient as he could have been with pesky fans. Producer William Frye observed one such incident during a lunch at the Brown Derby in Los Angeles. "As we were eating," he wrote in *Vanity Fair*, "a woman came up to the table, told him how much she loved his films, and he said, 'Do you have a dollar?' She said, 'What?' He repeated in his very metallic tone, 'Do you have a dollar?' That ended it—no dollar and no autograph."

That lunch took place in the late 1940s. But toward the end of his life, Grant would reflect on such incidents with regret. "I deplore the times I haven't been polite," he said. "I was impatient. I should have been more gracious with pushy fans."

The persistent incursions into Grant's private life by "pushy fans" (and the media) would have tested the patience of even the Dalai Lama. Still, he expected more of himself; he was not the kind of man to make excuses.

"They were gracious and patient in the face of constant harassment by people with cameras and autograph books."
— CG after meeting Douglas Fairbanks Sr. and Mary Pickford in 1920

But all that was behind him now. He was no longer at war with the world; he had transcended those troubles. Unlike other Hollywood icons—Elvis, Marilyn Monroe, James Dean, Marlon Brando—his life did not spiral downward. If anything the trajectory of his life was a steady ascent, both professionally and personally.

"He retired, remember," says Thomson, "at the top of his game, when he was still in demand, when many more paydays lay ahead. He could have milked it if he'd wanted to."

But he was tired, as he said, "of tripping over sound cords," tired of making films—seventy-two of them, in fact, that spanned decades of almost nonstop hard work. He'd had a daughter, Jennifer, in 1966 with his fourth wife, Dyan Cannon, and the discovery of paternal love had irrevocably changed him; it gave him the gift of a new and invigorating sense of purpose.

"If I had known then what I know now," he said, "if I had not been so utterly stupid or selfish. . . . I would have had a hundred children and I would have built a ranch to keep them on."

The movies were all fine and well, but Jennifer and Barbara were now his focus. They were what he called "real life." After all, the movies were just make-believe.

Although he did not become the victim of drugs or drink or even the most productive killer of them all—fame—holding it all together had come at a price.

"I don't call what I've been doing living. . . . I've been working since I was ten. I want to find out why I've been working. The answer can't be just to pay bills and to pile up more money and even if you do the government is going to take most of it. . . . I don't know what the answer is but I intend to find out; the world's changing out there. There are a lot of new exciting ideas running around. Some of them might be right and some might be cockeyed but they're affecting all our lives. I want to know how I stand, where I fit into the picture, what it's all going to mean to me. I can't find that out sitting behind some desk in an office, so as soon as I get enough money together I'm going to knock off for a while . . . quit . . . I want to save some of my life for myself."
— CG in *Holiday* (1938) with Katharine Hepburn

Just as his superstar status had demanded years of intense effort, so did the maturing of the inner man.

From 1960 to 1963, for instance, he'd benefited from a series of more than eighty therapeutic sessions with LSD, when it was still legal, to rid himself of what he described as his hypocrisies, nightmares, vanities, and the troubling events of his childhood. They had been supervised by a doctor trained in Freudian analysis, and while his friends might not have noticed a difference in him, he felt that the experience had been salutary.

"I learned," he said, "to forgive my parents for what they didn't know."

ISAIAH BERLIN once said, "Only barbarians are not curious about where they come from, how they came to be where they are, where they appear to be going, whether they wish to go there, and if so, why, and if not, why not."

Grant was still curious—about life, about himself, and about what lay ahead.

Unlike other Hollywood icons—Elvis, Marilyn Monroe, James Dean, Marlon Brando— his life did not spiral downward. If anything, the trajectory of his life was a steady ascent.

"Some people are totally at peace," he explained to a reporter in an interview over a meal in the mid 1980s, "but they are dead of course. I think of life as a series of plateaus. And since I hope to be on a better plateau, I can't say I'm completely satisfied. Do you see? Or have I ruined your lunch?"

The wit was still there, but a spiritual side of the man had emerged, and he channeled the same shrewd intellectual curiosity that had once been focused on creating a successful film persona into an evolution of a perhaps more meaningful nature.

Evidence of this can be found in his personal papers in a document marked "Meditation read by CG":

Now Lord you've known me a long time
You know me better than I know myself
You know that each day I am growing older and some day may even
be very old.

So meanwhile please keep me from the habit of thinking I must say
something on every subject and on every occasion. Release me from trying
to straighten out everyone's affairs. Make me thoughtful,
but not moody, helpful but not overbearing. I've a certain

CG and Joan Fontaine in Suspicion, *1941.*

amount of knowledge to share, still it would be very nice to have a few friends who, at the end, recognize and forgive the knowledge I lacked.

Keep my tongue free from the recital of endless details. Seal my lips on my aches and pains: they increase daily and the need to speak of them becomes almost a compulsion. I ask for grace enough to listen to the retelling of others' afflictions, and to be helped to endure them with patience. An embittered old person is a constant burden and a bore.

I would like to have improved memory, but I'll settle for humility and an ability to capitulate when my memory clashes with the memory of others. Teach me the glorious lesson that on some occasions I may be mistaken.

Keep me reasonably kind, considerate and genial. Please give me the ability to see good in unlikely places and talent in unexpected people.
And give me the chance to tell them so. Dear Lord.

ALTHOUGH THERE IS NO DEFINITIVE evidence that he underwent psychotherapy, the language Grant sometimes used suggests that he did or had at least read books that invited self-reflection. He often told friends who smoked that they should "like themselves better" and suggested that they quit.

At one point in his life, he developed an interest in the Chinese religion of Taoism because "you just go along with the rhythm of life."

Cary Grant in many ways was a modern man in step with the same issues and concerns that occupy us today. Cary Grant would have been right at home on *Oprah*.

MEN OF GRANT'S AGE are often preparing to depart this world, but he was just beginning to live. He had, thanks in large part to Barbara, reached an inner peace, a long-sought-after happiness in this, his fifth marriage.

"There was a serenity about him at eighty," says Bogdanovich.

Many men would have given up on love, become bitter and cynical after four divorces that had been sensationally chronicled in the media. In fact he had once stated that he would never marry again.

But Cary Grant had a resilient heart, an indomitable optimism. He was a very positive person. In the house he lived in he installed wide ramps for wheel-chair access, just in case he at some point would need them: he wanted to live a long, long life. His mother had lived to ninety-six.

It's a side of him that has gone unsung, unnoticed, perhaps because the outward persona was so appealing it eclipsed the true substance of the man. "Courage," wrote Amelia Earhart, "is the price life extracts for granting peace."

ANOTHER ASPECT of the photograph of Cary and Barbara reveals the couple's compatibility. It can be found in the way they mirror each other's taste and sensibility. Despite the age difference, one is as stylish as the other. They both share a preference for a classic rather than

Donald Spoto: "To Catch a Thief *was filmed in 1954, when Grant was 50. That year, Grace turned 25 and Jessie Royce Landis (above), who plays Grace's mother, was 49, some months younger than Grant. When Grant and Landis came to do* North by Northwest *in 1958, Hitch's assistant Peggy Robertson said about Landis, 'She doesn't look old enough to be Cary Grant's mother!' Hitch replied, 'Cary Grant has no age, so we only have to put a matronly fur piece on Jessie and everybody will accept her as Cary's mother.' And everybody believes it. He's ageless.*"

a trendy look. Barbara is wearing a dark skirt, a crisp white blouse underneath a dark sweater with a notched collar, and her lustrous brown hair is pulled back in a chignon. The look is as elegant and as appealing today as it was more than twenty years ago. Grant's is, too. He's also wearing dark slacks and a sweater with a notched collar.

Cary Grant looking very un–Cary Grant in Father Goose *(1964). But it was one of his favorite films.*

The sweater, though, is unusual. Like all of his clothes, it bears his unique stamp, even if it's only manifested in a small detail; the collar was modeled after one of his most admired garments.

"Nehru jackets are my favorite," he once remarked. "So comfortable, so practical. But, of course, the fashion industry would never allow them to stay. With a Nehru jacket a man didn't need a tie or a shirt or a jacket or cuff links, so a lot of money would be lost. Before I ever got around to buying one, they were gone."

So he had his cardigans made to his own specifications. Barbara also pitched in. She made him two caftans with that kind of collar. Barbara is now fifty-five but hasn't changed much since the photo was taken. She is youthful and slender, pretty-eyed, soigné, with a lively smile. Her hair is sun lightened but still lustrous, more golden than chestnut brown. Like Grace Kelly and Ingrid Bergman, two of Grant's favorite leading ladies, Barbara is a woman of natural beauty who still wears little or no makeup, one of the qualities that endeared her to her late husband, who first started tanning himself to avoid the messiness of greasepaint.

They seem harmoniously in tune on many levels, yet an unlikely pair on others. The age difference alone would have thwarted the efforts of the most ardent lovers. But it seemed to work for, rather than against, them.

"I was absolutely terrified by the forty-six-year age difference between us," Barbara recalled in *Cary Grant: A Touch of Elegance* by Warren G. Harris. "I thought—at great length—about the possibility of one day being without him. But I decided to go through with it because, otherwise, you don't have the time you do have, which is extremely precious."

But no relationship is perfect.

They argued. They argued a lot. Grant could be very stubborn; but Barbara could be just as stubborn, maybe even more stubborn.

But their tiffs didn't count for much. Not ultimately. What counted was the future, however long they had together.

Grant embarked on a national speaking tour in the 1980s called "A Conversation with Cary Grant." The couple traveled well together. They also laughed a lot. They had the same sense of humor.

Grant's motivation for agreeing to the tour was not an attempt to regain the spotlight after nearly twenty years of being out of it but an attempt, as he said, to "regain my self-confidence."

He also wanted to show Barbara, who had moved to the United States in 1978, the varied landscapes of the country he'd come to love.

"I know I'm overdoing it, going out night after night and traveling the country," Grant told a friend. "It totally drains me at times, but I'm not going to stop. I have to show Barbara and Jennifer I'm still young at heart."

And he did, exceeding his as well as their expectations. His tour was a huge success. All of the performances were sold out, and many of them ended with the audience giving him a rousing standing ovation.

The evenings began with a showing of an eight-minute film clip. The clips were mostly from his early movies because he found humor in the idea of the audience first seeing him in his younger days and then, when he walked out on stage, "incredibly aged," as he said.

A question-and-answer period followed that showed he was a razor-sharp septuagenarian, still in possession of his well-known ability to ad-lib. Unlike some actors he seemed to be at his best *without* a script. In the book based on these outings, Nelson's *Evenings with Cary Grant*, he reveals a multifaceted personality:

He could be witty:

How did you manage to look so good in North by Northwest *after being chased through open fields by a crop duster?*

CG: Six suits and dozens of ties.

He could be flirtatious:

What would you like for dinner if we were married?

CG: The way you say that, I'd probably skip dinner.

And he could be serious:

How does one achieve success?

CG: Diligence, perseverance, and enjoying what you do.

Although he had made his last film in 1966, he was as popular as ever. For the people who saw him in those small regional theaters, he was a legend come to life.

THE COUPLE MET in 1976 at a trade show for Faberge Cosmetics that was held at London's Royal Lancaster Hotel. Grant was Faberge's spokesperson, and Barbara worked in the hotel's Public Relations Department. Inevitably their paths crossed, but their first meeting was slightly less than auspicious.

Grant had arrived at the hotel with his longtime friend Roderick Mann, and they both noticed the exotic beauty who had been born in 1950 in Dar es Salaam, Tanzania (then Tanganyika), the daughter of Lesley and James Harris, a decorated World War II veteran of the Royal Army. Barbara had attended a boarding school in East Africa for ten years while her father worked as a provincial commissioner and continued her education when the family moved back to England, in 1960.

After she welcomed them to the hotel, she rushed off to a press conference. Grant was immediately smitten with not only the young woman's beauty but also her poise and intelligence. She at first refused their invitation to lunch because, as Mann put it, "she knew we were coming on to her."

But Grant's charm won her over, and she joined them for lunch. He also convinced her to attend Faberge's cocktail party that evening, but there was a mix-up. Mann came down to the lobby early. He was in one place; Grant was in another. When Barbara happened by, Mann asked her to join him for a drink before going on to the Faberge fete. Grant stumbled upon them having a cozy cocktail together and was incensed; he thought Mann was making an underhanded play for the woman he had already set his sights on. He coldly shunned his friend for three days. Mann eventually explained the situation, and all was forgiven.

In a gesture of reparatory friendship, Mann gave Grant a beautiful gold pen, which Barbara returned to him at Grant's request after his death.

Grant had fallen deeply in love again and began pursuing Barbara with a newfound vigor.

Grant's association with Faberge and Barbara's work at the hotel brought them together on future occasions, but the relationship soon progressed to another level. During the next two years, Grant made frequent trips to London to see Barbara socially. A friendship blossomed that soon turned romantic. Grant was seventy-four, Barbara twenty-eight.

"I never ever envisioned having any relationship other than a friendship with him," Barbara says in the documentary *A Class Apart*, "but because he was such an extraordinary individual, regardless of his age, I couldn't help myself. I couldn't stop from falling in love with him, and even though I knew that our time together would probably be limited, the quality of it was extraordinarily important to me, and I wouldn't have changed it for the world."

Barbara moved to America in 1978, where their relationship would undergo another test. Grant was concerned about how his young daughter, Jennifer, who was then twelve years old, would regard the new love of his life.

But he needn't have worried. The two hit it off immediately and remain close friends to this day.

On April 11, 1981, the couple married in a quiet ceremony on the terrace of Grant's Beverly Hills home, attended by a few family members and close friends. A more elaborate celebration was held over Easter weekend, at the home of Frank and Barbara Sinatra, where the newlyweds were joined by Veronique and Gregory Peck and Prince Rainier and Princess Grace, who were celebrating their twenty-fifth wedding anniversary.

Ever the romantic, Grant said he wanted to renew their wedding vows every five years.

THEIR MARRIAGE would remain strong, cemented by a lively enjoyment of each other's wit and sense of fun. They would often joke about their first fateful meeting at the Royal Lancaster in a way that evokes the affectionate banter typical of the films Grant starred in with Katharine Hepburn, Grace Kelly, and Audrey Hepburn. This exchange took place in front of a *GQ* reporter in 1986:

> "Yes," says Grant. "I saw a great deal of Barbara then. From ten-
> thirty in the morning till eleven."
> "When you were freeloading," she adds.
> "I just noticed this beautiful gal roaming around. She tried to avoid me."
> "That's not true," she insists.
> "The first time I saw you . . ."
> "I raced off to see Margaux Hemingway's press conference."
> "Yes, I was upstairs . . ."

Cary Grant and Samantha Egger in
Grant's final film, Walk, Don't Run, *1966.*

"No. You were downstairs, at the bar."

"Was I?"

"I thought you were quite a dish."

"A Conversation with Cary Grant" presented another opportunity for them to team up together. Barbara helped with the planning and travel arrangements so that Grant could concentrate on being Cary Grant.

Gregory Peck said that it was "a return to his roots. He'd played many of the same towns and theatres when he was Archie Leach."

Grant prepared for these appearances with the same diligence and attention to detail he brought to his wardrobe and film projects. Often before going on stage he would be wracked with nerves, but he always conquered his stage fright, and no one in the audience was the wiser.

Although it was work, it was work he loved, and he would align himself only with projects he enjoyed, especially after he retired from films. Reporters would frequently ask him why at his age he just didn't sit back, enjoy his wealth, or run off to Tahiti?

"This is my Tahiti," he told *New York Times* reporter Guy Flatley in 1973. "I don't put a great deal of effort into my work for Faberge. I get up in the morning, go to bed at night, and occupy myself as best I can in between. I do what I want when I want. Once, in St. Louis, I knew a fellow who ran a whorehouse, simply because it made him happy. Well, I do what makes me happy."

AND MAKING HIS FANS HAPPY made Grant happy. He insisted on the evenings being held at small regional theaters instead of big auditoriums. He also insisted that there was to be no advance publicity. He didn't want a big fuss, big crowds, or the pressure that came with big events. He preferred the intimate settings afforded by regional houses that reminded him of his old vaudeville haunts.

Grant insisted that the ticket price not exceed twenty-five dollars. That's what he felt it was worth and he wouldn't budge, even though he could have gotten ten times that amount or even more.

After the 1970 Hollywood Academy Awards presented him with a special Oscar for his lifetime achievement in film, the invitations poured in regularly for awards and honors, but he didn't enjoy public speaking. When the Kennedy Center offered to honor him in 1981, he agreed because he didn't have to make a speech.

But he was moved by all the attention and accolades, which often brought tears to his eyes. His friends kidded him about his sudden display of emotionalism and called him "Leaky Eyes."

But he remained the same modest man he'd always been. Rob Wolders recalls an incident that humorously illustrates Grant's lack of vanity, even after he'd firmly achieved iconic status.

"This happened in Washington, during the Ford administration," says Wolders, who was married at the time to actress Merle Oberon. He continues: "Queen Elizabeth came on a state visit, and President Ford invited a large number of mostly people with British backgrounds and some of the great artists and conductors who lived in the country. It was an extraordinary event and a white-tie event, the only one I've ever been to. And after the dinner, there was a dance where people milled around. At one point Merle and I were standing around talking to some people, and on the other side of the room there was Cary Grant, standing absolutely deserted; the most glamorous and the best-known man in the room was standing by himself.

"People somehow didn't dare to go up to him. He didn't invite it. He didn't emanate this social ease. And then he saw us across the room, and he started to come over, but in between where he was and where we were there was a podium on a set of risers with a small orchestra, and he started to come over but he suddenly realized that he would have to walk across those risers in order to get to us because the room was very crowded. As he stepped up on the riser, he realized that he was above all the other people, so he crouched, and he walked across the stage in a Groucho Marx duckwalk. It was one of the most amusing things I've ever seen. He went out of his way not to attract attention."

LIKE MANY of the theaters Grant appeared in during his tour, the one in Davenport, Iowa, was modest, charmingly creaky, and a far cry from the breathtakingly scenic locations of films like *To Catch a Thief.*

Grant and Barbara had arrived at the theater early, about three-thirty in the afternoon, to make sure everything was in place for Grant's Saturday evening appearance.

Right up until the end, he was a consummate professional, supervising every detail, from lighting to wardrobe.

Grant was in good spirits, joking with the staff and technical crew. Nothing seemed wrong. At least not yet.

He and Barbara had spent the earlier part of the day taking in the sights along the Mississippi River, stopping for lunch at a place coincidentally called Archie's, where they ate tasty grilled hot dogs and hamburgers. Grant considered the place a real "find."

"That morning he had been in great form," Barbara reports in *A Class Apart*. "We'd been walking around joking and having a wonderful time, and it was only that afternoon, when he was doing the rehearsal, that I understood something was going wrong because he could not focus."

Feeling ill, Grant wanted to go back to the hotel. He apologized profusely to everybody. Although he was gravely ill, he did not want to disappoint the people who had worked so hard preparing the event and the fans who had already bought tickets.

"I've never thought of Cary as being older than I am. I think of us a being the same age because he has a wonderful, facile mind. In many ways he is far more alive than I because he's so interested and vibrant."

—BARBARA GRANT

Grant's condition gradually worsened. Fearing a media fuss if he went to St. Luke's, the local hospital, the Grants went back to their hotel suite instead and called Dr. Gary Sugarman, his Los Angeles doctor, while local physicians tended to him. The news was not good. His blood pressure was dangerously high. Grant finally agreed to go to the hospital. Barbara remained at his side, comforting him, protecting him, talking to him.

The last photographs of Grant were taken at the theater during rehearsals. They show Barbara with her arms around him, his face not so much in pain but in a deep meditative state. He's impeccably dressed, in a dark blazer, checked shirt, and cuff links, his gray hair neatly combed—ever the showman, ready to walk out on stage.

But Cary Grant never did make that last appearance. He died later that night, at 11:22 p.m., on November 29, 1986, of a fatal stroke. His last words were, "I love you, Barbara."

HIS FRIENDS take some solace in the fact that he died as he had lived.

"He could have died at home in his bed, he could have died anywhere," Barbara remarked in *A Class Apart*, "but he was on the road, doing something that he loved to do."

When Cary Grant died, in 1986, director Billy Wilder and his wife, Audrey, sent Barbara Grant this telegram: "The model is gone. Who can we emulate now?"

But in many ways he's still with us, still a model, still an ideal worthy of our aspirations. For actors he is the gold standard by which they are measured. George Clooney, Hugh Grant, Jude Law, Pierce Brosnan, and even Mark Wahlberg have either been compared to or hailed as "the new Cary Grant." None, however, has measured up.

His influence extends beyond the narrow confines of Hollywood. He is part of the larger culture, exerting an influence in all areas of our lives. He is as much revered for the way he lived his life as for the films he made.

And in the fashion industry, he is a continual inspiration to new as well as established designers, including Ralph Lauren, Michael Kors, Richard Tyler, and Giorgio Armani.

NOW, TWENTY YEARS LATER, Barbara is happily married to business-man David Jaynes, a former NFL player and All-American quarterback at Kansas University, where he still holds the record for thirty-five career touchdown passes.

They have recently started a business together called Flight Maker, a private jet charter company that matches small groups of travelers who have common itin-eraries so they can share a plane without the expense of maintaining one of their own. Barbara and David divide their time between Los Angeles and Colorado.

For Barbara, letting go of the past wasn't always easy.

For two years, she cried every time she heard his voice.

But Grant wasn't a selfish man; he knew how important it was to love and to be loved.

He prepared her for the likely eventuality that he would die first and insisted, if that should happen, as it did, that she go on with her life.

The house, then, is not a shrine or a museum. It's a beautiful piece of real estate in a choice location that still offers some of the most scenic views in all of Beverly Hills. That's why Grant bought it in the first place, in 1946, a visionary even in the realm of real estate, and why Barbara retains ownership of it.

Still, she deftly honors his life while moving ahead with her own. When Grant's hometown of Bristol unveiled a statue of their native son in the town square in June of 2002, she attended the commemoration ceremonies with Jen-nifer. It was followed by a Cary Grant film festival that is now an annual event.

IN 1986, SHORTLY before his death, Barbara commissioned a special rose for her husband, a gift to him on Valentine's Day. Salmon colored to approximate his favorite color, orange, the flower is named the Cary Grant Rose. Hundreds of them thrived along the Grants' driveway and in their garden behind the kitchen. Grant's friend Prince Rainier planted them in his own garden in Monaco to honor Princess Grace, who had died in a car accident in 1982.

The roses still bloom. It's nice to think that they always will, suffused with sunshine, touched by ocean breezes, either on a hilltop in Beverly Hills or in a garden in Monaco or in some other peaceful place, adding color and beauty to the world, just like the man whom they were meant to honor.

May 30, 1980. Grant and wife Barbara attend a cocktail party for the opening of the remodeled Tiffany & Co. store in Beverly Hills.

CG STYLE: TIPS FROM THE MASTERS

"You could really be a Beau Brummel, baby, if you just give it half a chance."

—BILLY JOEL

There is nothing more repulsive than the slavish imitation of another man's style, but there's nothing wrong with picking up a few tips from the masters. After all, originality is a kind of artful plagiarism.

To begin, says Eva Marie Saint, "Clean out your closets."

Next comes the challenging part: take a hard, objective look at yourself. "Analyze yourself like an instrument," Audrey Hepburn once said. "You have to be absolutely frank with yourself. Face your handicaps, don't try to hide them. Instead, develop something else."

In the art of dressing well, you've heard it a million times: less is more. But in this increasingly cluttered world, it's worth repeating because as legendary *Vogue* editor Diana Vreeland said, "Elegance is refusal."

Samuel Goldwyn and many other studio bosses started out in the clothing trade. They recognized and admired a well-cut suit. Goldwyn refused to carry a single coin in his pocket because he felt even the slightest ripple or bulge would mar the cut of his immaculate suits. Cary Grant's Savile Row savvy was not only an expression of his personal style, it was a job requirement.

SUITS

Grant confessed that early in his career he had a penchant for flashy suits, "tweeds and Glenurquhart plaids." But his father, an employee of Tod's, the clothing manufacturer in England, set him straight. "My father said, 'Don't buy them because people will say, 'Here comes that suit down the road rather than Archie, which is me.'"

Never cease to learn from men of style. Even in his eighties CG was a shrewd observer of trends, noting of powerful men like Aristotle Onassis and super Hollywood agent Lew Wasserman, "those characters always wore dark-blue suits."

But dark suits, despite their ability to confer status and power, can seem bland and unhip. Obviate this unfortunate feature with a distinctive accessory. Ronald Winston, president of Harry Winston, Inc., jeweler to the stars, places a single diamond earring stud in the lapel of his suit jacket, a smart touch to what would otherwise be a staid look.

Savile Row's Carlo Brandelli goes the retro route by adding a fresh flower in the lapel of his killer Kilgour suits. He believes that black might be classic, but it can also be boring. Light up the dark with a carefully chosen accessory like the colorful Murano glass cuff links he designed especially for Kilgour (page 180).

Ronald Winston believes that you don't necessarily need to dress to kill, but you should dress to live. He wears a blazer or a suit jacket to breakfast even when he's dining alone. "It sets me up for my day."

Dress for success—and for loved ones.

John McClain, a drama critic in the 1960s and a man of style, said that "it is considerate to appear as soothing as possible for one's friends."

And reporters.

Author Tom Wolfe discovered that dressing well did more than just "set him up for his day." It set him up for a career.

"When I was being interviewed for my first book," he says, "I wasn't used to it. I was used to doing the interviewing because I was a journalist. I found that I didn't have much of a personality." So he let his clothes do the talking. Reporters focused on his eye-catching white suit rather than what he thought was his lack of a polished media persona. And that was fine with him. A trademark look was born and is still going strong forty years later. And so are his novels.

If you can't afford bespoke or even a top designer's off-the-rack suit, choose clothes that fit. CG liked the Brooks Brothers shirt and blazer, menswear staples in his day. Brooks Brothers is still a source for fine men's clothing. Find similar sources for inexpensive habiliments that offer a stylish as well as a flattering fit without the pain of a pricey purchase.

Well-dressed men (and women) select the best, but not necessarily the most costly, attire. An entry-level custom-made garment by a top-notch tailor costs about as much as some ready-made designer suits. You can look like a million without spending anywhere near that.

YOUR BEST FRIEND IS YOUR DRY CLEANER

Never dry-clean good suits. Dry cleaning gives them a cheap shine. If they're soiled have them spot cleaned at a dry cleaner you can trust. If they're just wrinkled have them pressed instead of dry-cleaned.

SHIRTS

Higher thread density gives fabric a softer, more luxurious feel.

CG cut the buttons off of his old shirts and jackets not because he was some kind of eccentric tightwad, but because they were special buttons. Look for buttons made from shell or some other high-quality material as opposed to plastic or metal.

Carlo Brandelli, creative director for Savile Row's Kilgour, was voted "Most Stylish Man" at the London GQ Awards 2005. Brandelli has personally worked with Bryan Ferry, Jude Law, and Hugh Grant, among other celebrities.

Founded in 1882, Kilgour includes as its clients Ava Gardner, Fred Astaire, Adnan Khashoggi, Joseph Kennedy, Robert Mitchum, Al Pacino, Noel Gallagher, Eric Clapton, Elton John, Emperor Akihito, and many leaders in the arts, politics, and industry.

French cuffs are distinctive, the mark of classic dressing. They also reference a more elegant era and provide a good reason to begin amassing a classy collection of cuff links. Start with simple but elegant black onyx or mother-of-pearl—and then go from there.

Brandelli designed the colorful cuff links pictured here. "They're made out of Murano glass," he says. "If you drop them, they might break. But I like that. It makes them precious."

TIES

You gotta have the CG dimple in the tie knot, even if you don't have a matching dimple in your chin. But keep the knots in proportion to your lapels and the size of your face, despite reigning trends.

COLOR

It's simple. Wear colors that contrast with your natural skin tone.

JEWELRY

Beau Brummel did not like jewelry. But times have changed. Still, the less jewelry the better. And if you must accessorize, accessorize with choice items. A good watch, a favorite pair of cuff links, a Tiffany tie clasp. Bling it on only if you're a rapper.

THE POWER OF STYLE

A sense of style based on one's own peculiar needs and features can transform the inner as well as the outer man. The poet John Keats knew this well. He said, "Whenever I find myself vaporish [sluggish], I rouse myself, wash and put on a clean shirt, brush my hair and clothes, tie my shoestrings neatly, and in fact Adonisize as if I were going out—then all clean and comfortable I sit back down to write. This I find the greatest relief."

Whether your goal is to be as fly as a rapper or as beautifully dressed as a Barclay's banker, individuality is the key. Think big, but start small. Learn the ins and outs of how to blend patterns. Start with simple checks and stripes to complement solid-colored suits or shirts. Then move on to plaids and pastels. When you feel really confident, push on to the paisleys, a tricky pattern that separates the man of style from what Tom Wolfe calls "the wet smacks."

"Style is confidence," says Amir, who has designed clothes for many confident men, including President Bill Clinton and Brad Pitt, as well as Cary Grant. CG wore an ascot as if it were a flower blossoming around his neck rather than just a bolt of silk stuffed down his shirt. Whatever you wear, wear it well. "Confidence," says Amir, "is what's really sexy."

CLOTHES AND FITNESS

Clothes can keep you fit. Quality clothes, that is. Packing on the pounds will result in a wanton waste of the money you spent on a quality wardrobe—just the thing to keep you on the StairMaster. Of course there are always alterations, but, hey, they cost money, too. And who has the time?

CELEBRATE

All situations are occasions to celebrate one's personal style. CG purchased a shearling vest with suede trim at a North Hollywood store to add a distinctive touch to the outfit he wore while horseback riding in Palm Springs. So whether it's a neighbor's barbecue or a Hamptons wedding, consult your inner style child for a creative and memorable look. You never know whom you might meet.

Never underestimate the power of the most seemingly trivial details to add style to your ensemble. CG insisted on his shirtsleeves extending no more than one quarter of an inch beyond his suit jackets. "Excellence is in the details," said architect Perry Paxton. "Give attention to the details and excellence will come."

SHOES

Nothing emasculates a man like sandals, flip-flops, or what Murray Kempton once called "those obscene ventilated shoes." Men have ugly feet. Even handsome men have ugly feet. Loafers, driving shoes, and moccasins like the kind CG wears in *To Catch a Thief* are smart alternatives for beach outings, resort visits, and yachting expeditions.

CG: "My father told me, 'If you can't afford good shoes, don't buy any. If you can afford one pair, buy black. If two pair, one black, one brown. But they must be good. Because even when they are old, they will always be seen to be good shoes.'"

LIFE

Style is more than how you wear your hat. It's also how you make your bed. Style should be deployed in all aspects of your life, from how you unbutton your button-down shirt to the way you create your correspondence. Pamela Clarke Keogh, author of *Jackie Style* and *Audrey Style*, likes the personal touch of handwritten letters on fine paper or elegant stationery because in a world of e-mail, Blackberries, cell phones, and instant messaging, communiqués with a personal touch stand out.

Put the style in lifestyle. Be modest, be cheerful, be positive, be charitable. Good manners are golden; they make you shine like a diamond pendant. Style isn't always about what you're wearing; it's about what you are.

CG in the United Artists wardrobe department preparing for battle in 1957's The Pride and the Passion.

"Style is the feather that helps the arrow fly, not the one you put in your hat."
—Stephen Bayley, art critic

WHAT I FIND FASCINATING about Cary Grant are the details of his personal style, how he grasped that it's the simple touches that create distinction. I like the way, for instance, he always manages a dimple in his tie knot, and the way his jackets always reveal a thrilling sliver of white shirtsleeve. He possessed that rare ability to be elegant but never foppish and to be impeccably turned out.

There was style in his demeanor as well. He maintained that enviably unruffled but always sympathetic debonair quality in all situations, even when he was on the run from bad guys in *North by Northwest*. And there was his subtle wit and humor, especially in his on-screen romantic encounters with Ingrid Bergman in films like *Indiscreet*, Katharine Hepburn in *Bringing Up Baby*, and Grace Kelly in the ultrastylish *To Catch a Thief*, perhaps the most stylish film of all time.

Few actors have shared the screen with so many of the twentieth century's most glamorous women—Marlene Dietrich, Ingrid Bergman, Myrna Loy, Grace Kelly, Sophia Loren, Eva Marie Saint, and Audrey Hepburn, to name a few.

But most of all, he had that gracious manner, that timeless elegance, on screen and off, that comes from the inner man, the true essence of style.

Although it's been twenty years since his death, forty years since he made his last movie, he still invites our awe and admiration, as a man, as an actor, and now here as a man of style.

He understood that the right clothes can confer authority and be a great source of pleasure and self-expression to the wearer. He was obviously a man who loved clothes, but he seems to have dressed for *us* because now the pleasure is all ours.

"Happy thoughts!"—CG

ACKNOWLEDGMENTS

MY HEARTFELT THANKS to Pamela Clarke Keogh, Steven Kent, Michael Sand, Rob Wolders, Amee Boyle, Giorgio Armani, Nacole Anzalone Snoep, Michael Kors, Tom Wolfe, David Thomson, Bob Willoughby, Donald Spoto, Eva Marie Saint, Carlo Brandelli, Oleg Cassini, Stephen Lachter, Alan Flusser, Ralph Lauren, Pamela Fiori, Peter Bogdanovich, Amir, Jack Taylor, Ronald Winston, Helen Gurley Brown, Wendy Schnee, Faye Thompson, Barbara Hall, Svend Petersen, Andrew Ramroop, Noel Uloth, Joel Avirom, Cynthia Cathcart, John Hassler, MD, Susan Redstone, Cynthia Dial, Denny Fallon, Vic Heman, the mighty Aztecs, and Tanqueray No. Ten.

Quotations throughout this book from Giorgio Armani, Michael Kors, Rob Wolders, Eva Marie Saint, Peter Bogdanovich, Tom Wolfe, David Thomson, Helen Gurley Brown, Oleg Cassini, Pamela Fiori, Alan Flusser, Bob Willoughby, Carlo Brandelli, Amir, Andrew Ramroop, Jack Taylor, Stephen Lachter, Donald Spoto, Noel Uloth, Ben Lane, Ronald Winston, Pamela Clarke Keogh, Svend Petersen, Nancy Nelson, and Barbara Grant Jaynes were drawn from original interviews conducted by the author.

PROLOGUE: A CELEBRATION OF STYLE

x   **overall sense of style as a designer,** Hollywood Life's *Movieline* magazine, November 2003.

xii   **For me, fashion doesn't stop,** Nathan T. Ellis, *"Time* Magazine Names Tom Ford America's Best Fashion Designer," Fashion Wire Daily, New York, July 2, 2001.

xvi   **I spent the greater part of my life fluctuating between Archie Leach and Cary Grant,** Grant, "Archie Leach," chapter one.

xvii   **If you wanted to be happy,** Lauren in *Cary Grant: A Class Apart,* documentary (Time Entertainment Co., 2004), produced, written, and directed by Robert Trachtenberg.

CHAPTER ONE: DRESSED TO KILL

6   **If he can talk,** West, *Goodness Had Nothing to Do with It,* 160.

7   **I welcomed any occupation,** Grant, "Archie Leach," chapter four.

7   **the seaside for a holiday,** Schickel, *Cary Grant,* 23.

7   **I realized at some point that she wasn't coming back,** Grant, "Archie Leach," chapter three.

7   **caused by "extreme toxicity,"** ibid.

7   **a slow breaking heart,** ibid.

7   **known to the world but not to my mother,** ibid.

7   **I was so often alone and unsettled,** ibid.

8   **the finest and largest troop in the area,** Grogan as quoted in Godfrey. *Cary Grant,* 29, 48, 49.

11   **We have recruited so much of the modern wardrobe,** Richard Martin, *Swords into Ploughshares: Military Dress and the Civilian Wardrobe,* Metropolitan Museum of Art, Costume Institute exhibition catalogue, 1995.

11   **Military dress is paradoxically,** ibid.

14   **Charles Eames, whose midcentury modern,** Eames as quoted in Pat Kirkham, *Charles and Ray Eames: Designers of the Twentieth Century* (Cambridge, MA: MIT Press, 1995).

SIDEBAR: HATS OFF AND BYE-BYE TO BOW TIES

15   *Esquire* **magazine once said,** Frazier, "The Art of Wearing Clothes."

21   **Grant caught the bow-tie bug from him,** Grant, "Archie Leach," chapter eight.

21   **the corniest habits in my attempt,** ibid.

CHAPTER TWO: THE AWFUL TRUTH

23   **As Jack Nicholson once said,** Jarski, *Hollywood Wit*, 179.

24   **a commercial failure and incited the American Association of Theatre Owners,** McCann, *Cary Grant*, 77.

24   **were snidely called "tuxedo romances,"** Eames, *The Paramount Story*, 92.

24   **I cultivated raising one eyebrow . . . dripped from nervous perspiration!** Nelson, *Evenings*, 68; also quoted in Harris, *Cary Grant*, 36; and Wansell, *Cary Grant: Haunted Idol*, 130.

25   **he was a work in progress,** *Cary Grant: A Class Apart*, documentary.

26   **barely able to manage, in his words,** Grant, "Archie Leach," chapter one.

27   **Those homemade trousers,** ibid., chapter three.

27   **Permit me to suggest that you dress neatly and cleanly,** ibid., chapter twelve.

29   **a proper little gentleman,** Wansell, *Cary Grant: Haunted Idol*, 23.

29   **at times he was downright wicked,** ibid., 38.

30   **I thought what a *marvelous* place,** Grant, "Archie Leach," chapter three.

30   **We lived and loved,** ibid.

30   **I often sat fascinated,** Grant, "Archie Leach," chapter two.

30   **His father advised him to purchase,** Elias Grant as quoted in Harris, *Cary Grant*, 181.

31   **Among the fellow passengers were newlyweds Douglas Fairbanks Sr.,** Grant, "Archie Leach," chapter five.

31   **a void in my life, a sadness of spirit,** ibid., chapter three.

31   **Although he described Mr. Leach,** ibid., chapter one.

31   **He was thirteen and awestruck,** ibid., chapter four.

32   **Pender had trained him and given him a job,** ibid.

35   **unfairly called "a fusspot,"** Thomson, *The New Biographical Dictionary of Film*, 353.

SIDEBAR: A TALE OF TWO (OR MAYBE THREE) JACKETS

36   **"He was very stiff,"** Betsy Drake in *Cary Grant: A Class Apart*, documentary.

36   **nervous perspiration he sometimes couldn't,** Nelson, *Evenings*, 68; also, Wansell, *Cary Grant: Haunted Idol*, 130.

37   **If a man's hand is in search of a jacket,** Flusser, *Dressing the Man*, 88.

CHAPTER THREE: STUDENT OF STYLE

41   **I patterned myself on a combination of Englishmen . . . an engaging answer for everything,** Nelson, *Evenings*, 68.

42 **"I love contrasting patterns/colors,"** Andre 3000 Benjamin, "International Best-Dressed List," *Vanity Fair*, April 2005, 205.

42 **"extra nuance of nattiness,"** original interview.

43 **"the staggering self-assurance,"** Vincent Canby, "*At Long Last Love* Evokes Past Films," *New York Times*, March 7, 1975.

44 **Grant called him "maddening but irresistible,"** Sidney Skolsky, *Tintypes*, syndicated column, 1934.

44 **In Cary's day you got nowhere—nowhere—with a lower-class accent,** Drake in *Cary Grant: A Class Apart*, documentary.

47 **In the late 1920s . . . puzzling accent,** Grant, "Archie Leach," chapter nine.

47 **Coward claimed that his habit of wearing flamboyant silk,** Hoare, *Noel Coward*, 140.

48 **I took to wearing coloured turtlenecked jerseys,** ibid.

48 **Cecil Beaton noted that "all sorts of men,"** Beaton as quoted in ibid.

48 **As Richard Rodgers noted,** Stephen Citron, *Noel and Cole: The Sophisticates* (New York: Oxford University Press, 1993), 223.

48 **inclination to ruin a correct ensemble by some flashy error of taste,** Coward as quoted in Hoare, *Noel Coward*, 140.

50 **Douglas Fairbanks Jr. followed in his father's fashionable footsteps,** Frazier, "The Art of Wearing Clothes."

50 **"Trust not,"** Carlyle as quoted in Tobias, *Obsessed by Dress*, 87.

50 **Hicks told Lonsdale that at such a time,** Seymour Hicks, *Between Ourselves* (London: Cassell and Co., 1930).

50 **My God, doesn't he know I haven't got long to live?** *Bartlett's Book of Anecdotes* (Boston: Little, Brown, 2000).

50 **Wit ought to be a glorious treat, like caviar,** Coward, *The Wit of Noel Coward* (London: Frewin, 1968).

50 **During rehearsals for one of his plays,** ibid.

50 **During a run-through of the revue "Sigh No More,"** ibid.

51 **Mae West told me she was working on a new play,** Cochran as quoted in Anton Bohm, *Literary Anecdotes* (Little Rock, AR: San Souci Press, 1963), 67.

51 **As Grant's fame grew,** Schickel, *Cary Grant*, 145.

52 **Ah, yes, that's quite true,** quoted in Frazier, "The Art of Wearing Clothes."

52 **"an incredible charmer,"** Kael, "The Man from Dream City," 8.

52 **He wasn't so much attracted to aristocrats,** Frasso in *Cary Grant: A Class Apart*, documentary.

53 **I might've starved that summer—or gone back to Bristol,** Grant, "Archie Leach," chapter eleven.

54 **I realized that to get anywhere in my work,** Grant in Nelson, *Evenings*, 59.

54 **Leach, who feels that acting in something by Johann Strauss calls for distinction,** critics Percy Hammond and Arthur Pollack quoted in Harris, *Cary Grant*, 43.

54   **The most intriguing toy I ever got my hands on,** Grant, "Archie Leach," chapter two.

54   **He said that he "remained deeply obliged" to his second wife,** ibid., chapter thirteen.

55   **He called her his "best piece of magic,"** Grant as quoted in McCann, *Cary Grant*, 85; also in Nelson, *Evenings*, 336.

55   **rather wooden,** *Cary Grant: A Class Apart*, documentary.

55   **not only studied their craft thoroughly and made films,** Grant, "Archie Leach," chapter six.

CHAPTER FOUR: FROM FLAWS TO FLAWLESSNESS

62   **adding that they thought he was "bow-legged and pudgy" to boot,** McIntosh and Weaver, *The Private Cary Grant*, 32.

62   **I don't think any non-actor,** Wansell, *Cary Grant: Haunted Idol*, 130.

63   **Long-necked men welcome the tab's higher positioning,** Flusser, *Dressing the Man*, 184.

72   **When I got to know Cary, he was the youngest eighty-year-old I'd ever met,** Lauren in *Cary Grant: A Class Apart*, documentary.

77   **At one time a two-pack-a-day smoker,** McIntosh and Weaver, *The Private Cary Grant*, 92; also in Donaldson and Royce, *An Affair to Remember*, 86.

78   **Cary looked marvelous that day,** Loy as quoted in Loy and Kotsilibas-Davis, *Being and Becoming*, 306.

79   **pants across the ocean,** Calloway and Jones. *Royal Style*, 191.

79   **but somewhat jokingly suggested that he should "dress better,"** Grant as quoted in Nelson, *Evenings*, 237.

79   **Once you know about it,** Wolfe, "The Secret Vice."

80   **Something of a maverick as to tailors,** Frazier. "The Art of Wearing Clothes."

SIDEBAR: A SUITABLE PROFESSION

81   **the line between the men and the boys in the art of wearing clothes,** Gingrich as quoted in ibid.

CHAPTER FIVE: ICON ASCENDING

85   **I like them because they're cooler than men's underwear,** Grant as quoted in Donaldson and Royce. *An Affair to Remember*, 63.

86   **They looked just like men's swimming trunks,** Donaldson as quoted in ibid.

87   **when Ryan returned after a tête-à-tête with the legendary actor,** Bogdanovich. *Who the Hell's In It?* 114.

87   **The magazine reported quite matter-of-factly,** Frazier. "The Art of Wearing Clothes."

88   **I was very fond of Ingrid . . . the amount of makeup she wears,** Grant as quoted in Shah, "Hul-LO." 94; also quoted in Nelson, *Evenings*, 149.

88   **I first saw the light of day,** Grant. "Archie Leach," chapter one.

88   **a chorus of crickets,** McIntosh and Weaver, *The Private Cary Grant,* 105.

88   **flattering but frustrating,** ibid.

88   **"looked artificial,"** ibid.

89   **the American male was the beneficiary,** Flusser, *Dressing the Man,* 8.

94   **To be really great in little things,** Stowe as quoted in Frazier, "The Art of Wearing Clothes."

96   **the incomparable set of his trousers spoilt,** Beerbohm as quoted in ibid.

96   **And if your hair falls out a bit,** Grant as quoted in Shah, "Hul-LO."

97   **One day he asked me to go,** Frye, "Gentlemen's Agreement."

97   **I always fancied shoes,** Grant as quoted in Shah, "Hul-LO."

97   **would rather be amiable and familiar with his tailor,** Prince of Wales as quoted in Frazier, "The Art of Wearing Clothes."

99   **Without a single noble, important, or valuable action to his credit,** Woolf as quoted in ibid.

99   **He didn't depend on his looks,** George Cukor in *Cary Grant: A Class Apart,* documentary.

CHAPTER SIX: AN INDEPENDENT MAN

105   **His expulsion was so unfair,** Charles Higham and Roy Moseley, *Cary Grant: The Lonely Heart* (Orlando, FL: Harcourt Brace Jovanovich, 1989), 20.

106   **I carefully watched the celebrated headline artists,** Grant, "Archie Leach," chapter five.

106   **The most prominent spire in the year of 1920,** Grant, "Archie Leach," chapter six.

108   **Today you cannot imagine the size of it,** Grant as quoted in Donaldson and Royce, *An Affair to Remember,* 152.

108   **The first thing I loved about America,** ibid.

110   **uncharming place,** Donaldson and Royce, *An Affair to Remember,* 135.

111   **I am writing to inform you Archie is coming home,** Pender as quoted in Nelson, *Evenings,* 34–35.

111   **Mrs. Pender has talked to him but it is no use,** ibid.

111   **It must have been very,** Grant, "Archie Leach," chapter eight.

112   **was called a "street fighter" by his third wife,** Drake in *Cary Grant: A Class Apart,* documentary.

113   **This handsome young man was always smiling,** Marx as quoted in Higham and Moseley, *Cary Grant,* 29.

113   **He took me to a preview of a movie,** Drake in *Cary Grant: A Class Apart,* documentary.

118   **Archie Leach has a strong masculine manner,** unidentified critic in Grant, "Archie Leach," chapter twelve.

119   **happily, gainfully, and steadily employed,** Grant, "Archie Leach," chapter twelve.

120 **"All the adventure, all the romance, all the excitement you lack,"** Gomery, *Shared Pleasures*, 63.

SIDEBAR: FASHIONABLE FURNISHINGS

121 **In his living room,** Shah, "Hul-LO."

CHAPTER SEVEN: A WAY WITH WOMEN

130 **As it was early spring,** Keogh, *Audrey Style*, 136.

132 **the blue jeans, the dope addicts, the Method,** Tom Wolfe, "The Secret Vice," *The Kandy-Kolored Tangerine-Flake Streamline Baby*, 170; also quoted in McGilligan, *Alfred Hitchcock*, 493.

132 **Audrey the aggressor . . . ultimately he was worn down by her,** Nelson, *Evenings*, 245.

133 **sex with civilized grace, sex with mystery,** Kael, "The Man from Dream City," 31.

134 **"It's as though," Hitchcock remarked, "she'd unzipped Cary's fly,"** Nelson, *Evenings*, 186.

135 **He had great curiosity,** Gregory Peck in *Cary Grant: Hollywood's Leading Man*, documentary (A&E Biography, Twentieth Century Fox Film Co., 1988).

142 **There isn't a thing wrong with you, old man,** Hitchcock as quoted in Harris, *Cary Grant: A Touch of Elegance*, 180.

142 **the kind folks at Levi's,** Grant as quoted in Mattlin, "Cary Grant in Palm Springs."

146 **Hitch and I had a rapport and understanding deeper than words . . . as well as he knew his own,** Nelson, *Evenings*, 217.

146 **According to Hitchcock biographer Patrick McGilligan,** McGilligan, *Alfred Hitchcock*, 490.

146 **went to work whistling,** Nelson, *Evenings*, 217.

147 **They carried on the fun,** *The Making of "To Catch a Thief,"* documentary (Paramount Pictures Home Video, 2002); also in McGilligan, *Alfred Hitchcock*, 499.

147 **I had this letter in my keyhole,** *The Making of "To Catch A Thief,"* documentary.

147 **so he would palm Grant off to John Michael Hayes, the screenwriter,** ibid.

148 **Well, Hitch . . . ,** DeRosa quoting Grant in *The Making of "To Catch a Thief,"* documentary.

148 **If he wanted me to wear something very specific he would tell me,** McGilligan, *Alfred Hitchcock*, 497.

154 **Grant seemed "to glow, to radiate masculine power perfectly deployed,"** Schickel, *Cary Grant: A Celebration*, 154.

155 **His romantic glamour, which had reached a peak in 1939,** Kael, "The Man from Dream City," 29.

SIDEBAR: TALL, DARK, AND VERY, VERY TAN

156 **"Archie Leach," he wrote, "has a mania for becoming browned . . ."** The Cary Grant Collection at the Margaret Herrick Library at the Academy of Motion Pictures Arts and

Sciences, Beverly Hills, CA, Manuscript Collection #94, Scrapbook #1 of 23, "Archie Leach" by Sidney Skolsky in *Tintypes*, a syndicated newspaper column.

157   Cary was dark-skinned naturally and took the sun very well, *Cary Grant: Leading Man,* documentary; also quoted in Nelson, *Evenings,* 292.

157   They look artificial, Shah, "Hul-LO."

CHAPTER EIGHT: ROMANTIC HEART

160   As we were eating, Frye, "Gentlemen's Agreement," 431.

160   I deplore the times I haven't been polite, Shah, "Hul-LO," 95.

160   pushy fans, Nelson, *Evenings,* 368.

160   If I had known then what I know now, Guy Flatley, "I Do What Makes Me Happy," *New York Times,* July 22, 1973.

160   They were what he called "real life," Godfrey, *Cary Grant,* 165.

162   to forgive my parents for what they didn't know, Shah, "Hul-LO."

162   Some people are totally at peace, Shah, "Hul-LO."

164   You just go along with the rhythm of life, Wansell, *Cary Grant: Haunted Idol,* 206.

167   Nehru jackets are my favorite, Shah, "Hul-LO."

167   I was absolutely terrified, Harris, *Cary Grant: A Touch of Elegance,* 250.

168   when he walked out on stage, "incredibly aged," Nelson, *Evenings,* 19.

172   Gregory Peck said, Harris, *Cary Grant: A Touch of Elegance,* 267.

174   His last words were, ibid., 3; also quoted in Nelson, *Evenings.*

SISEBAR: CG STYLE

178   Analyze yourself like an instrument, Keogh, *Audrey Style.*

178   Elegance is refusal, Vreeland, *D.V.*

178   Grant confessed that early in his career, Shah, "Hul-LO."

178   those characters always wore dark-blue suits, ibid.

178   it is considerate to appear as soothing as possible for one's friends, Frazier, "The Art of Wearing Clothes."

180   Whenever I find myself vaporish, Jay Tolson, ed., *Correspondence of Shelby Foote and Walker Percy* (New York: Doubletake/Norton, 1998).

181   Excellence is in the details, Paxton quoted in Historic Quotes and Proverbs Archives, World of Quotes.com.

181   those obscene ventilated shoes, Frazier, "The Art of Wearing Clothes."

181   My father told me, "If you can't afford good shoes," Shah, "Hul-LO."

Amies, Hardy. *The Englishman's Suit*. London: Quartet, 1994.

Anger, Kenneth. *Hollywood Babylon*. New York: Dell, 1981.

Archer, Eugene. "The Good Cary Grant." *New York Times*, August 22, 1965, sec. 2.

Bacon, James. *Hollywood Is a Four-Letter Word*. New York: Avon, 1976.

———. *Made in Hollywood*. New York: Warner Books, 1977.

Barton, Jane. "Cary Grant Wows Schenectady." *Variety*, July 18, 1984, 2, 149.

Berg, A. Scott. *Goldwyn: A Biography*. New York: Riverhead Books, 1989.

———. *Kate Remembered*. New York: Berkley Books, 2003.

Bergler, Edmund, MD. *Fashion and the Unconscious*. Madison, WI: International Universities Press, 1987.

Bergman, Ingrid, and Alan Burgess. *Ingrid Bergman: My Story*. New York: Delacorte Press, 1980.

Bogdanovich, Peter. "Cary Grant." In *Picture Shows*. London: George Allen & Unwin, 1975.

———. *Who the Hell's In It*. New York: Alfred A. Knopf, 2004.

Calloway, Stephen, and Stephen Jones. *Royal Style*. Boston: Little, Brown, 1991.

Cary Grant: A Class Apart. Documentary, 2004. Written, produced, and directed by Robert Trachtenberg; Turner Entertainment Co.

Cary Grant: Leading Man. Documentary, 1988. Written and produced by Gene Feldman and Suzette Winter; Wombat Production.

Cassini, Oleg. *In My Own Fashion*. New York: Pocket Books, 1990.

Chierichetti, David. *Edith Head: The Life and Times of Hollywood's Celebrated Costume Designer*. New York: HarperCollins, 2003.

Crowe, Cameron. *Conversations with Wilder*. New York: Alfred A. Knopf, 1999.

Curtis, Tony, and Barry Paris. *Tony Curtis: The Autobiography*. New York: William Morrow, 1993.

Davis, Debra Sharon. "Cary Grant: A Candid Conversation with America's Epitome of Elegance." *Playboy Guide: Fashion for Men, Spring–Summer*, 1981, 32.

Doherty, Thomas. *Pre-Code Hollywood: Sex, Immorality, and Insurrection in American Cinema, 1930–1934*. New York: Columbia University Press, 1999.

Donaldson, Maureen, and William Royce. *An Affair to Remember: My Life with Cary Grant*. New York: G. P. Putnam's & Sons, 1989.

Eames, John Douglas. *The Paramount Story: The Complete History of the Studio and Its 2,805 Films*. New York: Crown Publishers, 1985.

Ebert, Roger. *The Great Movies*. New York: Broadway Books, 2002.

Evans, Robert. *The Kid Stays in the Picture*. London: HarperCollins, 1994.

Fairchild, John. *Chic Savages*. New York: Simon and Schuster, 1989.

Fitzgerald, F. Scott. *The Great Gatsby*. New York: Scribner, 2004.

Fitzhenry, Robert I., ed. *The Harper Book of Quotations*. New York: HarperPerennial, 1993.

Flatley, Guy. "About Cary Grant—From Mae to September." *New York Times*, July 22, 1973, sec. 2.

Flocker, Michael. *The Metrosexual Guide to Style: A Handbook for the Modern Man.* Cambridge, MA: Da Capo Press, 2003.

Flusser, Alan. *Dressing the Man.* New York: HarperCollins, 2002.

———. *Style and the Man.* New York: HarperStyle, 1996.

Frazier, George Francis Jr. "The Art of Wearing Clothes." *Esquire*, September 1960.

Frye, William. "Gentlemen's Agreement." *Vanity Fair*, April 2003, 431.

Godfrey, Lionel. *Cary Grant: The Light Touch.* New York: St. Martin's Press, 1981.

Gomery, Douglas. *Shared Pleasures: A History of Movie Presentation in the United States.* Madison: University of Wisconsin Press, 1992.

Grant, Cary. "Archie Leach." *Ladies' Home Journal*, 3 parts, January/February, March, and April 1963.

Hack, Richard. *Hughes: The Private Diaries, Memos and Letters.* Beverly Hills, CA: New Millennium Press, 2001.

Hariman, Robert. *Political Style: The Artistry of Power.* Chicago: University of Chicago Press, 1984.

Harris, Warren G. *Cary Grant: A Touch of Elegance.* New York: Doubleday, 1987.

Hart, Moss. *Act One: An Autobiography.* London: Secker & Warburg, 1960.

Hoare, Philip. *Noel Coward: A Biography.* Chicago: University of Chicago Press, 1995.

Hotchner, A. E. *Sophia Living and Loving: Her Own Story.* New York: William Morrow, 1979.

Jarski, Rosemarie. *Hollywood Wit.* London: Prion, 2000.

Kael, Pauline. "The Man from Dream City." *When the Lights Go Down.* New York: Holt Rinehart Winston, 1980.

Kaminsky, Stuart. *Coop: The Life and Legend of Gary Cooper.* New York: St. Martin's, 1980.

Keegan, John. *The Mask of Command.* New York: Viking Penguin, 1987.

Keogh, Pamela Clarke. *Audrey Style.* New York: HarperCollins, 1999.

———. *Elvis Presley: The Man, The Life, The Legend.* New York: Atria, 2004.

Knowles, Elizabeth, ed. *The Oxford Dictionary of Twentieth Century Quotations.* New York: Oxford University Press, 1998.

Lewis, Adam. *Van Day Truex: The Man Who Defined Twentieth-Century Taste and Style.* New York: Viking Studio, 2001.

Loy, Myrna, with James Kotsilibas-Davis. *Myrna Loy: Being and Becoming.* New York: Bloomsbury, 1987.

Mann, Roderick. "Cary Grant: Doing What Comes Naturally." *Los Angeles Times*, June 11, 1978, calendar.

———. "Cary Grant at 80: Still a Touch of Mink." *Los Angeles Times*, January 15, 1984, calendar.

———. "Memories of Archie Leach." *Los Angeles Times*, December 2, 1986, calendar.

Mattlin, Everett. "Gary Grant in Palm Springs." *GQ*, March 1964.

McCann, Graham. *Cary Grant: A Class Apart.* New York: Columbia University Press, 1996.

McGilligan, Patrick. *Alfred Hitchcock: A Life in Darkness and Light.* New York: HarperCollins, 2003.

———. *George Cukor: A Double Life.* London: Faber, 1992.

McIntosh, William Currie, and William Weaver. *The Private Cary Grant.* London: Sidgwick & Jackson, 1983.

Nelson, Nancy. *Evenings with Cary Grant: Recollections in His Own Words and by Those Who Knew Him Best.* New York: Citadel Press, 2003.

Niven, David. *The Moon's a Balloon/Bring on the Empty Horses.* London: Coronet, 1985.

O'Brien, Glenn. *The Style Guy.* New York: Ballantine, 2000.

On Cukor. Documentary, 2002. Written and directed by Robert Trachtenberg; Turner Entertainment Co.

Paramount Homevideo, DVD: *To Catch a Thief, Widescreen Collection: Writing and Casting "To Catch a Thief"; The Making of "To Catch a Thief"; Alfred Hitchcock and "To Catch a Thief": An Appreciation; Edith Head: The Paramount Years Featurette.* 2002.

Ratcliffe, Susan, ed. *The Little Oxford Dictionary of Quotations.* New York: Oxford University Press, 1994.

Schickel, Richard, *Cary Grant: A Celebration.* New York: Applause Books, 1999.

Server, Lee. *Robert Mitchum: Baby, I Don't Care.* New York: St. Martin's, 2001.

Shah, Diane K. "Hul-LO, This Is Cary Grant." *GQ,* January 1986.

Spoto, Donald. *The Art of Alfred Hitchcock: Fifty Years of His Motion Pictures.* New York: Anchor Books, 1998.

———. *Camerado: Hollywood and the American Man.* New York: Plume, 1978.

———. *The Dark Side of Genius: The Life of Alfred Hitchcock.* New York: Da Capo Press, 1999.

Thomas, Bob. *King Cohn: The Life and Times of Hollywood Mogul Harry Cohn.* Beverly Hills, CA: New Millennium Press, 1967.

Thomson, David. *Movie Man.* New York: Stein and Day, 1967.

———. *The New Biographical Dictionary of Film.* New York: Alfred A. Knopf, 2002.

———. "Tall, Dark and Terribly Handsome." In *Movies of the Fifties.* Edited by A. Lloyd. London: Orbis, 1982.

———. *The Whole Equation: A History of Hollywood.* New York: Alfred A. Knopf, 2005.

Tobia, Tobi. *Obsessed by Dress.* Boston: Beacon Press, 2000.

Tolson, Jay, ed. *The Correspondence of Shelby Foote and Walker Percy.* New York: Doubletake/Norton, 1998.

Torregrossa, Richard. *The Little Book of Wisdom.* Deerfield Beach, FL: HCI, 1996.

Vreeland, Diana. *D.V.* Edited by George Plimpton and Christopher Hemphill. New York: Alfred A. Knopf, 1984.

Wansell, Geoffrey. *Cary Grant: Dark Angel.* New York: Arcade, 1996.

———. *Cary Grant: Haunted Idol.* London: William Collins Sons, 1983.

West, Mae. *Goodness Had Nothing To Do with It.* Englewood Cliffs, NJ: Prentice-Hall, 1959.

Wolfe, Tom. "The Secret Vice," *The Kandy-Kolored Tangerine-Flake Streamline Baby.* New York: Bantam, 1999.

Zilkha, Bettina. *Ultimate Style: The Best of the Best Dressed List.* New York: Assouline, 2004.

Zukor, Adolph, with Dale Kramer. *The Public Is Never Wrong.* New York: G. P. Putnam's Sons, 1953.

Every reasonable effort has been made to acknowledge the ownership of copyrighted photographs and documents included in this volume. Any errors that have inadvertently occurred will be corrected in subsequent editions provided notification is sent to the author.

Courtesy of the American Academy Motion Pictures Arts & Sciences, Paramount Collection: *Houseboat* (Paramount, 1958), still 007782/Metro-Goldwyn-Mayer Collection: *North by Northwest* (Metro-Goldwyn-Mayer, 1959), still 007781/Production files; *Holiday* (Columbia, 1938), still D-COL-17-46/CG Biography files; Grant, Cary, 8 stills: CG-39, CG-54, CG-161, CG-162, D-COL-17-113, LM228406, 007695, 007696 (Metro-Goldwyn-Mayer Collection); *North by Northwest* (Metro-Goldwyn-Mayer, 1959), still 007781/Paramount Collection; *Houseboat* (Paramount, 1958), still 007782/Production files; *Holiday* (Columbia, 1938), D-COL-17-46/CG Biography files; Grant, Cary, CG-39, CG-54, CG-161, CG-162, D-COL-17-113, LM28406, 007695, 007696/Cary Grant Collection; *The Awful Truth* (Columbia, 1937), still 8416; *The Grass Is Greener* (Universal-International, 1961), No. 6/8; *Hot Saturday* (Paramount, 1932), No. 8670; *Houseboat* (Paramount, 1958), Nos. 8669, 8668; *Notorious* (RKO Radio, 1946), No. 8414; *The Pride and the Passion* (United Artists, 1957), Nos. 8664, 8667 8665, 8666; *That Touch of Mink* (Universal International, 1962), No. 8663, 1916-5AD/Paramount Collection; *Hot Saturday* (Paramount, 1932), No. 907-91/The RKO Collection; *Notorious* (RKO, 1946), CG-R-137, 141, N-Pub-A9, A55, A66, N-R-12, 47, N-ADV-74, 79, N-11, 33, 36, 37, 126; *Suspicion* (RKO, 1941), BT-Pub A7, A18, A26, 49, 74, 120/John Truwe Collection: *North by Northwest* (MGM, 1959), No. 8662/United Artist Collection: *The Pride and the Passion* (United Artist, 1957), No. 8661, P-R235a, 390A/Production files; *Charade* (Universal, 1963), 1928-IAD, 1928–50; *Father Goose* (Universal, 1964), 1944–35; *Indiscreet* (U.K., Warner Bros., 1958), No. 106A/Cary Grant Collection: Biography, env. Nos. 34, 81, 172, 308, 106/Production files; *Blonde Venus* (Paramount, 1932), RS#9; *Madame Butterfly* (Paramount, 1932), No. 912-135; *North by Northwest* (MGM, 1959), Nos. 1743–44, 1743–57; *To Catch a Thief* (Paramount, 1955), Nos. 11511–2/59, 11522–74, R003P025.

Courtesy of and © 1961 Bob Willoughby: Chapter Seven, photos 1–4 of CG with Margo McKendry.

Courtesy of and © 1985 The Richard Torregrossa Collection: Chapter Eight, color photo of Cary Grant and Barbara Grant.

Courtesy of Kilgour: photographs of Carlo Brandelli in "Cary Grant Style: Tips from the Masters." © 2005 by Sean Ellis.

Courtesy of Jerry Ohlinger, Inc., New York: Prologue, CG in *The Grass Is Greener* (Universal-International, 1959), CG and Irene Dunne in *Penny Serenade* (Columbia, 1941), CG in *Suspicion* (RKO, 1941); Chapter One, CG in *Suspicion* (RKO, 1941); Chapter Two, *The Awful Truth* movie card (Columbia, 1941), CG and Katharine Hepburn in *Holiday* (Columbia, 1938), CG in *Charade* (Universal-International, 1963), CG in polka-dot tie; Chapter Three, Noel Coward/Douglas Fairbanks Sr., CG & Eva Marie Saint in *North by Northwest* (MGM, 1959); Chapter Four, CG in towel, *That Touch of Mink* (Universal-International, 1962), CG in *Indiscreet* (Warner Bros., 1958), CG in *To Catch a Thief* (Paramount, 1955), CG in *Toast of New York* (RKO, 1932); Chapter Five, CG haircut on the set of *The Grass Is Greener* (Universal-International, 1961); Chapter Six, CG and Barbara Hutton, and CG, Martha Hyer, and Sophia Loren in *Houseboat* (Paramount, 1958); Chapter Seven, *Charade* movie card (Universal-International, 1963), CG on set, CG and Brigitte Auber in *To Catch a Thief* (Paramount, 1955), Movita, CG, Deborah Kerr in *Dream Wife* (MGM, 1953), CG and Eva Marie Saint in *North by Northwest* (MGM, 1959), CG in *North by Northwest* (MGM, 1959), Grace Kelly in *To Catch a Thief* (Paramount, 1955), CG and Grace Kelly on set of *To Catch a Thief*

(Paramount, 1955), CG and Suzy Parker in *Kiss Them for Me* (20th Century-Fox, 1957), *Charade* movie card (Universal-International, 1963), CG on set of *To Catch a Thief* (Paramount, 1955); Chapter Eight, *Suspicion* (RKO, 1941), CG and Katharine Hepburn in *Holiday* (Columbia, 1938), CG in robe on the set of *Charade* (Universal-International, 1963), "A Friend in Need," CG and Audrey Hepburn in *Charade* (Universal-International, 1963), Merle Oberon, *Charade* movie card (Universal-International, 1963); "Fashionable Furnishings," CG in glider, CG at piano in *Night and Day* (Warner Bros., 1946), CG and Eva Marie Saint in *North by Northwest* (MGM, 1959), CG in "sack suit"; "Hats Off and Bye-Bye to Bow Ties," CG in elevator, *North by Northwest* (MGM, 1959), CG confronting men in *North by Northwest* (MGM, 1959), CG and crop duster in *North by Northwest* (MGM, 1959); "Tall Dark and Very, Very Tan," CG tan, CG under sunlamp in *The Awful Truth* (Columbia, 1937); "CG Style: Tips from the Masters," CG with helmet on set of *The Pride and the Passion* (United Artists, 1957).

style of, 165–67

Grant, Cary (Archibald Alexander Leach):
    accent and speech patterns of, 44–45
    acting career of. *See also specific movies*
        acting abilities and, 23, 36
        as contract player at Paramount, 3–6, 14,
            16, 23–24, 32, 55, 103–4, 120
        desire for independence and, 104, 120
        in musical comedies, 53–54, 61, 117–19
        screen test for Paramount and, 61–62, 120
        start of, 53–54, 116–20. *See also* vaudeville
    aircraft of, 122–23, *123*
    birth of, xii
    British role models of, 41–51
    business acumen of, 53, 55–56
    charitable works of, 8–10, 135–42
    charming personality of, 27–29, 128–30
    childhood of, xii–xiv, 7–9, 26–27, 29–30,
        31, 75, 89, 104–5
    death of, 174–75
    as escort for society women, 52, 114
    facial features of, 15
    fans' rapport with, 160
    fearless independence of, 104, 110, 120
    hair of, 16, 52, 72, 96
    hand in pocket as signature gesture of,
        24–25, 32, *36*, 36–39, *37*
    health and fitness of, 31, 72–78
    homes of:
        in Beverly Hills, *121*, 121–22, 175
        Santa Monica beach house, 4, 74, 76
    influence of, xi, xii
    lively curiosity and learning of, 54–55
    LSD therapy sessions undergone by, 79,
        162
    name changed by, ix
    national speaking tour of (*A Conversation
        with Cary Grant*), 56, 168, 172, 173
    as necktie salesman, 114
    in Pender's team of comic acrobats (Knock-
        about Comedians), 30, 31–32, 44, 52,

        104–11, 116
    personal growth of, 162–64
    personal transformation of, xiv–xvi, 24–25,
        30–35, 41–55, 72–75, 114
    physical flaws of, 61–66, 68–72
        bow-leggedness, 62, 72
        broad neck, 62–66, *64, 65*, 68–69
        hair parted on right rather than left, 72
        irregularly placed teeth, 69–72, *73*
        large head, 63–64, *65*
        narrow sloping shoulders, 63–64
        pudginess, 62, 72–74
    piano playing of, 123
    punctuality of, 109
    retirement of, xii, 134–42, 160
    romantic life of, 75–76, 130
        affair with Sophia Loren, 77, 140
        marriage to Barbara Harris, 159, 164,
            165–72
        marriage to Barbara Hutton, 106–8
        marriage to Dyan Cannon, 29, 160
        marriage to Virginia Cherrill, 76
        on-screen romances and, 128–34, 150–52
    rose named after, 176
    rumored to be gay, 23, 24
    sartorial style of, xv–xvi, 78–99
        awareness of physical flaws and, 61–66,
            68
        bow ties and, *20*, 21
        casual look and, 66–67, 81–82, 142
        childhood experiences and, 26–27, 30, 89
        experimentation and, 21
        Fairbanks's influence on, 30–31, 32, 41
        hats and, 15–17
        investment in men's apparel shop and, 78
        jackets and, 36–39
        mixing patterns and, 32, 42
        neckerchiefs and, *60*, 66, 67, *67*
        neckties and, 18, 28, 29, 32, 34, 63, 87,
            180
        Nehru jackets and, 167